I0447058

Private Means, Public Ends:
Voluntarism vs. Coercion

Edited by J. Wilson Mixon, Jr.

The Foundation for Economic Education, Inc.
Irvington-on-Hudson, New York

Large Print Edition published 2012 by Skyler J. Collins.
Visit: www.skylerjcollins.com

Cover image by StockFreeImages.com.

ISBN-13: 978-1480012080
ISBN-10: 1480012084

Table of Contents

Introduction by J. Wilson Mixon, Jr.   1

I. THE OPTIONS: FREEDOM OR COERCION

Planning in a Free Society   9
   Henry Hazlitt

II. THE ESSENTIALS OF SOCIETY:
LANGUAGE, ART, COMMUNICATION

A Tale of Two Dictionaries   21
   John P. Finneran

Art and Representative Government   25
   William R. Allen and William Dickneider

Art and Commerce   28
   Barbara Dodsworth

In Praise of Billboards   33
   Lawrence Person

Kosher Kops   36
   Jacob Sullum

Telecompetition: The Free Market and the Road to the Information Superhighway: A Review   41
   Raymond J. Keating

Regulation of Telecommunications   44
   Clint Bolick

III. A CARING SOCIETY: HEALTH, EDUCATION,
AND WELFARE WITHOUT COERCION

Home Schooling: A Personal Experience   57
   Hannah Lapp

A School with a Money-Bank Guarantee   62
   Scott Payne

The Generosity of Americans: A Review   66
    Richard Christenson

The Tragedy of American Compassion: A Review   68
    Daniel Bazikian

Charity in the Land of Individualism   72
    John D. Fargo

Ending Welfare as They Know It   75
    Gerald Wisz

The Best for Priscilla   78
    Robert A. Peterson

Friendly Societies: Voluntary Social Security and—More   81
    John Chodes

Lodge Doctors and the Poor   87
    David T. Beito

IV. BASES OF A DYNAMIC ECONOMY

The Forgotten Private Banker   99
    Richard Sylla

Free Market Money in Coal-Mining Communities   106
    Richard H. Timberlake

The Growth of Privatized Policing   119
    Nicholas Elliott

Taking the Train to Metamora   124
    William B. Irvine

Private Highways in America, 1792-1916   128
    Daniel B. Klein

Socialism, U. S. Style   134
    Henry Hazlitt

New York's War Against the Vans   136
    Robert Zimmerman

A Species Worth Saving   140
    John Kell

V. EPILOGUE: FREEDOM, THE *SINE QUA NON*

What Makes a Market?   145
    Ross C. Korves

Introduction

Richard Cornuelle recalls how Americans addressed problems before every perceived need became an excuse for government intervention: "We wanted, from the beginning, a free society, free in the sense that every man was his own supervisor and the architect of his own ambitions. . . . We wanted, as well, with equal fervor, a good society—a humane, responsible society in which helping hands reached out to people in honest distress, in which common needs were met freely and fully. . . . We built a much wider array of new institutions for this purpose than we built to insure political freedom. . . . People joined together in bewildering combinations to found schools, churches, opera houses, co-ops, hospitals, to build bridges and canals, to help the poor."[1]

The potpourri that is human action is even more varied: This quotation leaves out market-directed actions. Private interactions create a virtual wildflower field. Not every flower is perfect, but the overall effect is breathtaking. Government meddling often entails poisoning the ground, then lamenting its inability to produce, and finally setting out a few very expensive potted plants. The natural field fades from memory. Critics decrying the "planned" display's ugliness and expense face the rebuttal that, at least, the government's offerings are in place whereas alternatives are hypothetical, even fanciful. (Who, having never seen one, could envision a field of wildflowers?)

1. Making the Case for Private Action

In 1965, Leonard Read captured the dilemma facing proponents of noncoercive private responses to "social" problems. "Ask the average successful businessman, 'Should mail delivery be left to the free market?' Unable to think how he would deliver mail to nearly 200 million people, unable to *design or engineer* the project in his own mind—that is, being unaware of how the market really works—he will likely draw the socialistic conclusion: 'Of course not. Mail delivery is a job for government.' The businessman can no more figure out how to deliver the mail than you or I can blueprint the dismantling of socialism or the unscrambling of an egg."[2]

Read then sketches the market system's logic, "millions of 'this-for-thats,' in a chaos which defies cataloguing." This apt depiction underscores the free-market proponent's dilemma: Most public-policy analysts cannot or will not delve into the market's logic deeply enough to appreciate the power of private action.

Concrete examples of private provision for "social" wants lighten the proponent's burden. Arguing for free-market mail delivery in 1995 rather than 1965 is a much easier task. Federal Express and UPS, along with E-mail and dismissive references to "snail mail," make the prospect real. Examples demonstrate the pertinence of free-market principles. Unfortunately, though, socialistic enterprise tends to displace the private activity that would have (and perhaps had) provided the benefits claimed for socialism. Where socialism persists long enough, the memory of privately-provided service vanishes.

The Freeman has presented cases of private individuals doing for themselves and for each other things that planners assert must be done in the public (read: coercive) sector. These articles show how human action, when free of governmental meddling, produces a good society.

Principles precede cases. Henry Hazlitt compares "economic planning" and the free market. Would-be planners see the private sector, he says, as "a world of chaos and anarchy, in which nobody ever planned ahead or looked ahead." "Planners" complain that uncoerced individual action leads either to the wrong things being provided or not enough being provided. To rectify this, agents of the public (coercive) sector must restrict the actions of the private (voluntary) sector. The resulting welfare state is Bastiat's "great fiction in which everybody tries to live at the expense of everyone else." Hazlitt concludes, and the articles that follow illustrate, that "within the framework of the market economy, the institution of private property, and the general rule of law, we will all improve our economic condition much faster than when we are ordered around by bureaucrats." Private (voluntary) means best serve public ends (the ends of a community).

2. Communication: Language, Art, and Commerce

Language is essential for the success enjoyed by the human species. Yet the state has done little to build or design it. Where government has intruded, the results are not auspicious. After languages had evolved spontaneously for centuries, scholars began to standardize grammar and spelling. French scholars formed the French Academy; its product, half a century in the making, was ponderous, pompous, and formalistic. Samuel Johnson, recognizing that "Custom is the most certain mistress of language," produced in seven years a masterpiece that still affords pleasure and illumination.

As humans' prosperity depends on language, our spiritual welfare demands artistic expression. From prehistoric times, masterworks have expressed our hopes and fears. Today, a chorus chants that having a healthy artistic community requires government participation. Following the Israelites who would be "like the nations" (I Samuel 8:19), they claim that virtually every government has supported the arts. In truth, however, art has flourished largely as a commercial endeavor and, for much of America's history, without significant taxpayer support. Further, whatever other governments have done, forcing taxpayers to fund favored artistic projects is not consistent with the ideals of representative government.

Language and art are the bases for human communication. In a free society, communication often combines persuasion and information. For consumers to use information or to react to persuasion, they must have freedom to choose. A prevailing prejudice is that consumers cannot handle this freedom, so regulators must restrict communication in order to protect them. This prejudice demeans consumers and ignores the wealth of information routinely distributed through private channels.

New technologies bring communication to public attention and place it in regulators' cross-hairs. Private initiatives develop new technologies that make communication easier and less costly. Regulations deny us the full benefits of these innovations. For example, the government created a system of exclusive broadcast licenses, claiming that the spectrum is inherently limited. Cable television soon revealed the claim's fallacy, but was regulated anyway. Deregulation would mean than license holders could no longer gain from monopoly grants. Even so, the communications revolution continues, despite regulators, because free minds design and implement ways around barriers, natural or governmental.

3. Education and Welfare within Communities

An essential component of communication is imparting knowledge and insights to succeeding generations. From the beginning, America's settlers educated their young. Until the late nineteenth century, parents bore the responsibility for this crucial task, often helped by church or community organizations. Government involvement, when present, was local and limited. Many better-educated citizens, like Thomas Edison, learned at home; today 300,000 to 500,000 students follow this path. Both home schooling and the growth of private schools reflect dissatisfaction with the government schooling that, following the "reforms" of Horace Mann and others, displaced approaches that had served for centuries.

Educating its children is a hallmark of a community; another is caring for its disadvantaged. Here, the state has been involved for some time, often with troubling results. Olasky relates Benjamin Franklin's distress over England's Poor Laws:

> There is no country in the world in which the poor are more idle, dissolute, drunken and insolent. The day you passed that act you took away from before their eyes the greatest of all inducements to industry, frugality and sobriety. . . . Repeal that law and you will soon see a change in their manners. St. Monday and St. Tuesday will cease to be holidays.[3]

Franklin's insight guided private charity for over a century, a period unparalleled for the proliferation of privately financed schools and colleges, hospitals, orphanages, and many other benevolent institutions. Acts of compassion and caring were idiosyncratic and arbitrary, but they worked. They worked because they distinguished between the deserving poor and paupers, and because people were treated as individuals, not as ciphers.

The needy depend on voluntary acts of others. All suffer life's vicissitudes. Mostly, we deal with these by planning. We buy insurance, save, live within a supporting family, and enter into other private arrangements to protect us from the unexpected. Before government intruded, the range of private responses was much greater. One especially important but largely forgotten institution was the friendly society. These societies did not just provide mutual aid; they also secured services for their members. In particular, before the organized medical profession used state power to end the practice, "friendlies" often procured medical care at favorable rates by contracting with lodge doctors.

4. Facilitating Private Exchange

Banking, at the heart of a private exchange system, evolved without government calling it into existence. Rather, once banks were in place, government enforced monopoly positions and exacted favors in return, weakening the private sector. Even as government restricts banks' ability to serve the needs of commerce, other private options evolve. Retailers offer layaway options and credit. Employers provide short-term credit. An instructive example of the private sector persevering to provide banking services despite government restrictions is the widespread use of scrip in mining communities for half a century.

Banking provides the financial infrastructure for exchange. Physical infrastructure and institutional infrastructure likewise facilitate private interactions. Modern governments claim a central role in providing "infrastructure"—a word elastic enough to include "investments" in higher education. The claim that government must provide highways and dams, and police and court systems, typically rests on the neoclassical "public goods" doctrine. Despite prevailing acceptance, the case is far from compelling. Even police and judiciary services are often effected without coercion.

Policing is almost universally accepted as an appropriate government activity, but much of the business of establishing and enforcing rules of conduct has always been private. Reliance on private substitutes for an unsatisfactory judiciary has been increasing for some time. Private mediation, arbitration, or other alternative methods of dispute resolution frequently displace traditional court functions. The private sector also provides a growing share of police services. The effectiveness of private policing and judiciary activities despite heavily subsidized government alternatives suggests that assertions that the market cannot provide "public goods" are ex post justifications for government activities.

The case for government dominance in transportation is even weaker. Early on, the American republic relied on private or local government initiatives for transportation. During the first three decades of the nineteenth century, for example, turnpike construction—executed primarily by townships—added some 10,000 miles to our highways. This undertaking, relative to the economy's size, exceeded post-World War II highway construction.[4] A less apparent, but equally important aspect of private construction is that the boom abated when other alternatives (mainly steamboats and railroads) evolved.

Most transportation involves short distances, especially within cities. Here, government's dead hand has relentlessly restricted private initiative. Since the 1910s, city governments have granted urban transportation monopolies in return for part of the proceeds. Despite regulators' efforts to maintain government-created monopolies, however, privately-produced transportation serves many citizens, often the most needy.

As with "infrastructure," it is a commonplace that government must protect the environment from private interests. This article of faith ignores government damage to the environment, both directly and by destroying private individuals' incentives to conserve. Here again, private initiative more reliably safeguards environmental quality than do sentimental statements by political rulers. This is true for the well-being of North American wolves and for East African elephants. Incentives to protect and enhance the environment lead more predictably to desired results than do hectoring and commanding.

5. Summing Up

After generations of expanding government, many forget that society need not depend on government for its "public" goods and services. Most can be, and have been, produced without coercion. Private action occurs within a staggering array of institutions, integrated by the market mechanism. Individuals and communities of individuals, working sometimes in their own interests and sometimes as altruists, build a society largely independent of governmental ministrations.

J. Wilson Mixon
Dana Professor of Economics
Berry College

---

1. Richard C. Cornuelle, *Reclaiming the American Dream: The Role of Private Individuals and Voluntary Associations* (New Brunswick: Transactions Publishers, 1993) , p. 21.

2. Leonard E. Read, "Unscrambling Socialism," *Essays on Liberty,* Vol. 12, 1965, p. 465.

3. Marvin Olasky, *The Tragedy of American Compassion* (Washington D.C.: Regnery Gateway, 1992), p. 43.

4. Gerald Gunderson, "Privatization and the 19th-Century Turnpike," *Cato Journal,* Spring/Summer 1989, p. 192.

I. THE OPTIONS:
FREEDOM OR COERCION

"Planning" vs. the Free Market

by Henry Hazlitt

When we discuss "economic planning," we must be clear concerning what it is we are talking about. The real question being raised is not: plan or no plan? but *whose* plan?

Each of us, in his private capacity, is constantly planning for the future: what he will do the rest of today, the rest of the week, or on the weekend; what he will do this month or next year. Some of us are planning, though in a more general way, ten or twenty years ahead.

We are making these plans both in our capacity as consumers and as producers. Employees are either planning to stay where they are, or to shift from one job to another, or from one company to another, or from one city to another, or even from one career to another. Entrepreneurs are either planning to stay in one location or to move to another, to expand or contract their operations, to stop making a product for which they think demand is dying and to start making one for which they think demand is going to grow.

Now the people who call themselves "Economic Planners" either ignore or by implication deny all this. They talk as if the world of private enterprise, the free market, supply, demand, and competition, were a world of chaos and anarchy, in which nobody ever planned ahead or looked ahead, but merely drifted or staggered along. I once engaged in a television debate with an eminent Planner in a high official position who implied that without his forecasts and guidance American business would be "flying blind." At best, the Planners imply, the world of private enterprise is one in which everybody works or plans at cross purposes or makes his plans solely in his "private" interest rather than in the "public" interest.

Now the Planner wants to substitute his *own* plan for the plans of everybody else. At best, he wants the *government* to lay down a Master Plan to which everybody else's plan must be subordinated.

Henry Hazlitt (1894–1993), noted economist, author, editor, reviewer, and columnist, was well known to readers of the *New York Times, Newsweek, The Freeman, Barron's, Human Events,* and many other publications. Best known of his books are *Economics in One Lesson, The Failure of the "New Economics," The Foundations of Morality,* and *What You Should Know About Inflation.* This article originally appeared in the December 1962 issue of *The Freeman.*

It Involves Compulsion

It is this aspect of Planning to which our attention should be directed: Planning always involves *compulsion*. This may be disguised in various ways. The government Planners will, of course, try to persuade people that the Master Plan has been drawn up for their own good, and that the only persons who are going to be coerced are those whose plans are "not in the public interest."

The Planners will say, in the newly fashionable phraseology, that their plans are not "imperative," but merely "indicative." They will make a great parade of "democracy," freedom, cooperation, and non-compulsion by "consulting all groups"—"Labor," "Industry," the Government, even "Consumers Representatives"—in drawing up the Master Plan and the specific "goals" or "targets." Of course, if they could really succeed in giving everybody his proportionate weight and voice and freedom of choice, if everybody were allowed to pursue the plan of production or consumption of specific goods and services that he had intended to pursue or would have pursued anyway, then the whole Plan would be useless and pointless, a complete waste of energy and time. The Plan would be meaningful only if it forced the production and consumption of *different* things or different quantities of things than a free market would have provided. In short, it would be meaningful only insofar as it put compulsion on *somebody* and forced some change in the pattern of production and consumption.

There are two excuses for this coercion. One is that the free market produces the *wrong* goods, and that only government Planning and direction could assure the production of the "right" ones. This is the thesis popularized by J. K. Galbraith. The other excuse is that the free market does not produce *enough* goods, and that only government Planning could speed things up. This is the thesis of the apostles of "economic growth."

The "Five-Year Plans"

Let us take up the "Galbraith" thesis first. I put his name in quotation marks because the thesis long antedates his presentation of it. It is the basis of all communist "Five-Year Plans" which are now aped by a score of socialist nations. While these Plans may consist in setting out some general "overall" percentage of production increase, their characteristic feature is rather a whole network of specific "targets" for specific industries: there is to be a 25 percent increase in steel capacity, a 15 percent increase in cement production, a 12 percent increase in butter and milk output, and so forth.

There is always a strong bias in these Plans, especially in the communist countries, in favor of heavy industry, because it gives increased power to make war. In all the Plans, however, even in noncommunist countries, there is a strong bias in favor of industrialization, of heavy industry as against agriculture, in the belief that this necessarily increases real income faster and leads to greater national self-sufficiency. It is not an accident that such countries are constantly running into agricultural crises and food famines.

But the Plans also reflect either the implied or explicit moral judgements of the government Planners. The latter seldom plan for an increased production of cigarettes or whisky, or, in fact, for any so-called "luxury" item. The standards are always grim and puritanical. The word "austerity" makes a chronic appearance. Consumers are told that they must "tighten their belts" for a little longer. Sometimes, if the last Plan has not been too unsuccessful, there is a little relaxation: consumers can, perhaps, have a few more motor cars and hospitals and playgrounds. But there is almost never any provision for, say, more golf courses or even bowling alleys. In general, no form of expenditure is approved that can not be universalized, or at least "majoritized." And such so-called luxury expenditure is discouraged, even in a so-called "indicative" Plan, by not allowing access by promoters of such projects to bank credit or to the capital markets. At some point government coercion or compulsion comes into play.

"The Nation" Cannot Afford It

This disapproval and coercion may rest on several grounds. Nearly all "austerity" programs stem from the belief, not that the person who wants to make a "luxury" expenditure cannot afford it, but that "the nation" cannot afford it. This involves the assumption that, if I set up a bowling alley or patronize one, I am somehow depriving my fellow citizens of more necessary goods or services. This would be true only on the assumption that the proper thing to do is to tax my so-called surplus income away from me and turn it over to others in the form of money, goods, or services. But if I am allowed to keep my "surplus" income, and am forbidden to spend it on bowling alleys or on imported wine and cheese, I will spend it on something else that is not forbidden. Thus when the British austerity program after World War II prevented an Englishman from consuming imported luxuries, on the ground that "the nation" could not afford the "foreign exchange" or the "unfavorable balance of payments," officials were shocked to find that the money was being squandered on football pools or dog races. And there is no reason to suppose, in any case, that the "dollar shortage" or the "unfavorable balance of payments" was helped in the least. The austerity program, insofar as it was not enforced by higher income taxes, probably cut down potential exports as much as it did potential imports; and insofar as it was enforced by higher income taxes, it discouraged exports by restricting and discouraging production.

But we come now to the specific Galbraith thesis, growing out of the agelong bureaucratic suspicion of luxury spending, that consumers generally do not know how to spend the income they have earned; that they buy whatever advertisers tell them to buy; that consumers are, in short, boobs and suckers, chronically wasting their money on trivialities, if not on absolute junk. The bulk of consumers also, if left to themselves, show atrocious taste, and crave cerise automobiles with ridiculous tailfins.

Bureaucratic Choice

The natural conclusion from all this—and Galbraith does not hesitate to draw from it—is that consumers ought to be deprived of freedom of choice, and that government bureaucrats, full of wisdom—of course, of a very *un*conventional wisdom—should make their consumptive choices for them. The consumers should be supplied, not with what they themselves want, but with what bureaucrats of exquisite taste and culture think is good for them. And the way to do this is to tax away from people all the income they have been foolish enough to earn above that required to meet their bare necessities, and turn it over to the bureaucrats to be spent in ways in which the latter think would really do people the most good—more and better roads and parks and playgrounds and schools and television programs—all supplied, of course, by government.

And here Galbraith resorts to a neat semantic trick. The goods and services for which people voluntarily spend their own money make up, in his vocabulary, the "private sector" of the economy, while the goods and services supplied to them by the government, out of the income it has seized from them in taxes, make up the "public sector." Now the adjective of "private" carries an aura of the selfish and exclusive, the inward-looking, whereas the adjective "public" carries an aura of the democratic, the shared, the generous, the patriotic, the outward-looking—in brief, the public-spirited. And as the tendency of the expanding welfare state has been, in fact, to take out of private hands and more and more take into its own hands provision of the goods and services that are considered to be most essential and most edifying—roads and water supply, schools and hospitals and scientific research, education, old-age insurance, and medical care—the tendency must be increasingly to associate the word "public" with everything that is really necessary and laudable, leaving the "private sector" to be associated merely with the superfluities and capricious wants that are left over after everything that is really important has been taken care of.

If the distinction between the two "sectors" were put in more neutral terms—say, the "private sector" versus the "governmental sector," the scales would not be so heavily weighted in favor of the latter. In fact, this more neutral vocabulary would raise in the mind of the hearer the question whether certain activities now assumed by the modern welfare state do legitimately or appropriately come within the governmental province. For Galbraith's use of the word "sector," "private" or "public," cleverly carries the implication that the public "sector" is legitimately not only whatever the government has already taken over but a great deal besides. Galbraith's whole point is that the "public sector" is "starved" in favor of a "private sector" overstuffed with superfluities and trash.

Voluntary versus Coercive

The true distinction, and the appropriate vocabulary, however, would throw an entirely different light on the matter. What Galbraith calls the "private sector" of the economy is, in fact, the *voluntary* sector; and what he calls the "public sector" is, in fact, the *coercive* sector. The voluntary sector is made up of the goods and services for which people voluntarily spend the money they have earned. The coercive sector is made up of the goods and services that are provided, regardless of the wishes of the individual, out of the taxes that are seized from him. And as this sector grows at the expense of the voluntary sector, we come to the essence of the welfare state. In this state nobody pays for the education of his own children but everybody pays for the education of everybody else's children. Nobody pays his own medical bills, but everybody pays everybody else's medical bills. Nobody helps his own old parents, but everybody else's old parents. Nobody provides for the contingency of his own unemployment, his own sickness, his own old age, but everybody provides for the unemployment, sickness, or old age of everybody else. The welfare state, as Bastiat put it with uncanny clairvoyance more than a century ago, is the great fiction by which everybody tries to live at the expense of everybody else.

This is not only a fiction; it is bound to be a failure. This is sure to be the outcome whenever effort is separated from reward. When people who earn more than the average have their "surplus," or the greater part of it, seized from them in taxes, and when people who earn less than the average have the deficiency, or the greater part of it, turned over to them in handouts and doles, the production of all must sharply decline; for the energetic and able lose their incentive to produce more than the average, and the slothful and unskilled lose their incentive to improve their condition.

The Growth Planners

I have spent so much time in analyzing the fallacies of the Galbraithian school of economic Planners that I have left myself little in which to analyze the fallacies of the Growth Planners. Many of their fallacies are the same; but there are some important differences.

The chief difference is that the Galbraithians believe that a free market economy produces too much (though, of course, they are the "wrong" goods), whereas the Growthmen believe that a free market economy does not produce nearly enough. I will not here deal with all the statistical errors, gaps, and fallacies in their arguments, though an analysis of these alone could occupy a fat book. I want to concentrate on their idea that some form of government direction or coercion can by some strange magic increase production above the level that can be achieved when everybody enjoys economic freedom.

For it seems to me self-evident that when people are free, production tends to be, if not maximized, at least optimized. This is because, in a system of free markets and private property, everybody's reward tends to be equal the value of his production. What he gets for his production (and is allowed to keep) is in fact what it is worth in the market. If he wants to double his income in a single year, he is free to try—and may succeed if he is able to double his production in a single year. If he is content with the income he has—or if he feels that he can only get more by excessive effort or risk—he is under no pressure to increase his output. In a free market everyone is free to maximize his satisfactions, whether these consist in more leisure or in more goods. But along comes the Growth Planner. He finds by statistics (whose trustworthiness and accuracy he never doubts) that the economy has been growing, say, only 2.8 percent a year. He concludes, in a flash of genius, that a growth rate of 5 percent a year would be faster! How does he propose to achieve this?

What Rate of Growth

There is among the Growth Planners a profound mystical belief in the power of words. They declare that they "are not satisfied" with a growth rate of a mere 2.8 percent a year; they demand a growth rate of 5 percent a year. And once having spoken, they act as if half the job had already been done. If they did not assume this, it would be impossible to explain the deep earnestness with which they argue among themselves whether the growth rate "ought" to be 4 or 5 or 6 percent. (The only thing they always agree on is that it ought to be greater than whatever it actually is.) Having decided on this magic overall figure, they then proceed either to set specific targets for specific goods (and here they are at one with the Russian Five-Year Planners) or to announce some general recipe for reaching the overall rate.

But why do they assume that setting their magic target rate will increase the rate of production over the existing one? And how is their growth rate supposed to apply as far as the individual is concerned? Is the man who is already making $50,000 a year to be coerced into working for an income of $52,500 next year? Is the man who is making only $5,000 a year to be forbidden to make more than $5,250 next year? If not, what is gained by making a specific "annual growth rate" a governmental "target"? Why not just permit or encourage everybody to do his best, or make his own decision, and let the average "growth" be whatever it turns out to be?

The way to get a maximum rate of "economic growth"—assuming this to be our aim—is to give maximum encouragement to production, employment, saving, and investment. And the way to do this is to maintain a free market and a sound currency. It is to encourage profits, which must in turn encourage both investment and employment. It is to refrain from oppressive taxation that siphons away the funds that would otherwise be available for investment. It is to allow free wage rates that permit and encourage full employment. It is to allow free interest rates, which would tend to maximize saving and investment.

The Wrong Policies

The way to *slow down* the rate of economic growth is, of course, precisely the opposite of this. It is to discourage production, employment, saving, and investment by incessant interventions, controls, threats, and harassment. It is to frown upon profits, to declare that they are excessive, to file constant antitrust suits, to control prices by law or by threats, to levy confiscatory taxes that discourage new investment and siphon off the funds that make investment possible, to hold down interest rates artificially to the point where real saving is discouraged and malinvestment encouraged, to deprive employers of genuine freedom of bargaining, to grant excessive immunities and privileges to labor unions so that their demands are chronically excessive and chronically threaten unemployment—and then to try to offset all these policies by government spending, deficits, and monetary inflation. But I have just described precisely the policies that most of the fanatical Growthmen advocate.

Their recipe for inducing growth always turns out to be—inflation. This does lead to the *illusion* of growth, which is measured in their statistics in monetary terms. What the Growthmen do not realize is that the magic of inflation is always a short-run magic, and quickly played out. It can work temporarily and under special conditions—when it causes prices to rise faster than wages and so restores or expands profit margins. But this can happen only in the early stages of an inflation which is not expected to continue. And it can happen even then because of the temporary acquiescence or passivity of the labor union leaders. The consequences of this short-lived paradise are malinvestment, waste, a wanton redistribution of wealth and income, the growth of speculation and gambling, immorality and corruption, social resentment, discontent and upheaval, disillusion, bankruptcy, increased governmental controls, and eventual collapse. This year's euphoria becomes next year's hangover. Sound long-run growth is always retarded.

In Spite of "The Plan"

Before closing, I should like to deal with at least one statistical argument in favor of government Planning. This is that Planning has actually succeeded in promoting growth, and that this can be statistically proved. In reply I should like to quote from an article on economic planning in the *Survey* published by the Morgan Guaranty Trust Company of New York in its issue of June 1962:

"There is no way to be sure how much credit is due to the French plans in themselves for that country's impressive 4 1/2 percent average annual growth rate over the past decade. Other factors were working in favor of growth: a relatively low starting level after the wartime destruction, Marshall Plan funds in the early years, later an ample labor supply siphonable from agriculture and from obsolete of inefficient industries, most recently the bracing air of foreign competition let in by liberation of import restrictions, the general dynamism of the Common Market, the break-through of the consumer as a source of demand. For the fact that France today has a high degree of stability and a strong currency along with its growth, the stern fiscal discipline applied after the devaluation of late 1958 must be held principally responsible.

"That a plan is fulfilled, in other words, does not prove that the same or better results could not have been achieved with a lesser degree of central guidance. Any judgment as to cause and effect, of course, must also consider the cases of West Germany and Italy, which have sustained high growth rates without national planning of the economy."

In brief, statistical estimates of growth rates, even if we could accept them as meaningful and accurate, are the result of so many factors that it is never possible to ascribe them with confidence to any single cause. Ultimately we must fall back upon an a priori conclusion, yet a conclusion that is confirmed by the whole range of human experience: that when each of us is free to work out his own economic destiny, within the framework of the market economy, the institution of private property, and the general rule of law, we will all improve our economic condition much faster than when we are ordered around by bureaucrats.

II. THE ESSENTIALS OF SOCIETY:
LANGUAGE, ART, COMMUNICATION

A Tale of Two Dictionaries

by John P. Finneran

For many centuries, the English and the French languages, lacking formally binding rules, evolved spontaneously, inconsistently, and idiosyncratically. With the advent of the Enlightenment, attempts were made to end this state of linguistic anarchy by standardizing grammar and spelling, most notably through the creation of grammar books and dictionaries. This article deals with two of the most notable of the early dictionaries: the French dictionary created by the French Academy (*l'Académie française*) and the English dictionary created by Samuel Johnson.

The two dictionaries were completed in different ways and at different speeds: the English dictionary was composed by a single man in seven years; whereas the French dictionary was composed by a body of 40 members in agonizingly slow 55 years. This fact seems bizarre at first; many people, by dividing the work amongst themselves, surely *should* have been able to complete roughly the same task that one man was engaged in in *less* time than it took that one man. Yes, Samuel Johnson was a genius, but the French Academy also had its share of geniuses; even if we were to make the wild assumption that Samuel Johnson had the mental powers of ten Academicians, Johnson would still have been outnumbered by four to one; so surely genius alone cannot explain the vast anomaly. I suggest that much of the contrast can be explained by the ineluctable differences inherent in a collective, government-sponsored effort and in one that is individual and profit-making.

The French Dictionary

The French Academy was established in 1635 by King Louis XIII. The charter of the Academy stated: "There will be composed a dictionary, a grammar, a rhetoric, and poetics under the observation of the Academy."[1] Thus officially began the project for the French dictionary. Work began in earnest in 1639 under the direction of Claude Favre de

Mr. Finneran is a writer from Marshfield, Massachusetts. This article originally appeared in the December 1992 issue of *The Freeman*.

Vaugelas. Work was extremely slow and problematic. Indeed, the Academy spent six years (*i.e.*, almost as long as it took Johnson to complete his entire dictionary) working solely on the letter "G." The dictionary appeared at last in 1694.

The 55 years were characterized by, in the words of W. L. Wiley, "ponderous slowness . . . empty pomposity and . . . wasted formalistic interchanges."[2] This atmosphere was best captured by Antoine Furetière in the following satiric depiction of the workings of a committee of Academicians, which, alas, sounds all too true:

> The one who shouts the loudest is the one who is right; each person gives forth with a long harangue on the slightest trifle. The second man repeats like an echo everything that the first has said, and most frequently three or four of them talk at the same time. In the commission composed of five or six persons, there is one of them who reads, one who offers his opinion, two who chat, one who sleeps, and one who spends his time perusing some dictionary which is on the table. When it is the turn of the second to express his views, the article has to be read to him again because of his distraction during the first reading. . . . No two lines are accepted without long digressions, without somebody telling a funny story or a tidbit of news, or without somebody else talking about conditions in the country and about reforming the government.[3]

Antoine Furetière was a member of the Academy who was expelled from that body for working on a rival dictionary. He produced his dictionary in 1690, four years ahead of the Academy. According to Wiley, Furetière's dictionary "has in general been regarded by posterity as a fuller and more usable instrument than the Academy's dictionary."[4] The Academy accused Furetière of plagiarism and of infringing on the Academy's monopoly on the production of a French dictionary. Furetière vigorously denied both charges, claiming that he had been working independently on his dictionary for 20 years and that he had a rival monopoly. After completing his dictionary, Furetière spent his remaining days writing stinging satire that excoriated the inefficiencies of the Academy.

The English Dictionary

Samuel Johnson had his own problems in producing his dictionary, most notably concerning patronage, or, rather, the lack thereof. Johnson dedicated the plan of his dictionary to Philip Dormer, Lord Chesterfield, in the hope of enticing the latter's financial support. But, save for the negligible sum of ten pounds, such hope was in vain. Lord Chesterfield offered substantial help only when the project was virtually completed. Johnson haughtily refused the belated offer.

Johnson, who, among his other talents, was an accomplished poet, had produced the following couplet in imitation of Juvenal:

Yet think what ills the scholar's life assail,
Pride, envy, want, the *garret*, and the jail.

Johnson's unhappy experience with patrons caused him to change the second line to:

Toil, envy, want, the *Patron*, and the jail.[5]

The financing of Johnson's dictionary came from local booksellers—and here we have one of the great factors speeding Johnson along: Johnson's need to pay back the booksellers, who would profit from the sale of the completed dictionary. Johnson had spent entirely the booksellers' money before he completed the project and, as an affair of honor, he felt compelled to prevent his financiers from suffering a loss. The sheer immensity of the work caused Johnson to take seven years at the task instead of the expected three, but, by working by himself, Johnson was able to avoid all of the "wasted formalistic interchanges" that so bedeviled the Academy. The fact that Johnson worked alone also gave the dictionary a distinctly *individual* flavor. (To be punctilious: Although, for all practical purposes, it is fair to say that Johnson worked alone, he did have six mechanical assistants, and 20 etymologies were provided by Zachary Pierce, the bishop of Rochester.) Johnson's *Dictionary of the English Language* was completed in 1755.

Johnson's dictionary had its share of blunders and omissions, but can still be read profitably today as much for its sparkling of personality and wit as for its formal applications. Here are some examples of Johnson's definitions: *network:* "Anything reticulated or decussated, at equal distances, with interstices between the intersections;"[6] *oats:* "A grain, which in England is generally given to horses, but in Scotland supports the people"[7] (A Scotsman is said the have replied, "Yes, which is why England had the best horses in the world, and Scotland has the best people."); *abbey-lubber:* "A slothful loiterer in a religious house, under pretense of retirement and austerity;"[8] *pension:* "An allowance given to any one without equivalent. In England it is generally understood to mean pay given to a state hireling for treason to his country;"[9] and, my favorite, to *fishify*: "To turn to fish: a cant phrase."[10]

A Poetic Summation

The history of the two dictionaries can be summed up by two verses. The first is Furetière's suggested epigram for the French Academy's dictionary:

> I am this big dictionary,
> Which was for half a century in the belly of my mother;
> When I was born I had a beard and some teeth;
> This fact should not be considered very unusual;
> Since I was at the time fifty years old.[11]

The second is David Garrick's reaction to the publication of Johnson's dictionary (although the difference he attributes to national character, I suggest really should be attributed to the difference between individuals and collective bodies):

> Talk of war with a Briton, he'll boldly advance,
> That one English soldier will beat ten of France,
> Would we alter the boast from the sword to the pen,
> Our odds are still greater, still greater our men . . .
> [after citing Shakespeare, Milton, Dryden, and Pope]
> And Johnson, well arm'd like a hero of yore,
> Has beat forty French, and will beat forty more![12]

---

1. W.L. Wiley, *The Formal French* (Cambridge, Mass.: Harvard University Press, 1967), p. 89.

2. *Ibid.*, p. 93.

3. *Ibid.*, pp. 93–94. Wiley comments (p. 94), "With due allowance for Furetière's likely bias, it sounds as though he might have attended such a committee meeting."

4. *Ibid.*, p. 94.

5. James Boswell, *Life of Johnson* (New York: Oxford University Press, 1970), pp. 186–187.

6. Samuel Johnson, *Johnson's Dictionary: A Modern Selection*, edited by E.L. McAdam, Jr., and George Milne (New York: Pantheon Books, 1963), p. 263.

7. *Ibid.*, p. 268.

8. *Ibid.*, p. 33.

9. *Ibid.*, p. 288.

10. *Ibid.*, p. 181.

11. Wiley, p. 94.

12. Boswell, pp. 214–215.

Art and Representative Government

by William R. Allen and William Dickneider

There, on a patio of a university campus, was a pile of twisted, rusted iron pipe. But it wasn't debris from plumbing renovation. It was an art exhibition.

Why had the artist blessed us with this miniature junkyard? It was neither pretty to the eye nor coherent to the mind. Of course, we are not to ask what a modern painting or sculpture *is*. But perhaps it is legitimate to ask what the artist meant to *convey*.

If we generously presume that the artist is really saying something of importance, how are we to receive and translate the message? Are we to suppose that the message sent is the same as the message received? If not, this is peculiar and clumsy communication. Or maybe no message is being sent although one is to be received, with the receiver doing the artist's work by inferring something that wasn't transmitted.

Perhaps interaction between producer and consumer isn't the intended game, at all. Maybe the purpose of the artist is personal catharsis: by dumping rusted pipe on the patio, he gets a psychological monkey off his back. Or maybe it is to be a profitable variation of "the emperor's clothes" scam, with a clientele of connoisseurs finding art where lesser folk see only junk.

Within broad limits—if the art community is to be subject to any constraints—surely "producer sovereignty" should prevail, with individual artists determining the nature of their own creations. But let there be also "consumer sovereignty" in consumption of the art produced. Let consumers determine for themselves the works of art they pay for. Further, don't restrict philanthropists in subsidizing artists: one of the tenets of a system of markets and private property is that people generally can dispose of their assets as they please.

But two points of elaboration.

First, while artists are to be free to use resources which either they *buy* with their earned income or which are *given* to them by private

Dr. Allen is Professor of Economics Emeritus at UCLA; he and William Dickneider collaborate on the *Midnight Economist* radio program, syndicated by the Reason Foundation of Santa Monica, California. This article originally appeared in the November 1991 issue of *The Freeman*.

patrons, they have no right to *commandeer* resources from unwilling contributors through exploiting the coercive powers of government.

Second, we are not morally obliged either to subsidize or to deify artists. While we guard the freedom to create works of art—even piles of twisted, rusted pipe—protecting artistic freedom is very different from insisting that taxpayers buy whatever people choose to produce with that freedom.

But some artists, like some of the rest of us, can be seduced by government favor and applause. "The arts are not a luxury," says a lawmaker, "they are the soul of society." Art "reflects things that are happening in our society," says another, "and closing our eyes will not make these things go away. Such art can help us recognize other influences on our culture and even help us understand them. And if it does not help me or you specifically, you can be sure that it is helping someone, somewhere, who can relate to it."

Artists are not loath to accept an exalted role. ". . . art is social conscience," we are assured by the director of a subsidized theater. "Art," he says, "has only one obligation—to tell stories and make images about who and what we are and who and what we might become." In all the community, "only the artist must tell the truth."

Such precious rationalization for raids on the Treasury cannot be analytically persuasive. Better to acknowledge simply that beneficiaries want the money and politicians want their support—and to remember that the arts flourished for most of America's history without substantial federal money. Only in the last few decades has government put arts significantly on the dole.

Government is not the wellspring of art and culture. Nor does some law of nature or sense of social survival compel us to clutch sensitive artistic souls as our conscience, guide, or judge. Subsidizing artists is not a role of government that is clearly legitimate or even commonly accepted. All except addled anarchists acknowledge that government *does* have reason for being. Most agree that government properly provides such fundamental services and arrangements as law and order and administration of justice, national defense, and protecting property rights which conduce economic efficiency and social stability.

But something like subsidization of the arts is an alien element in this context. It is not a "public good" like national defense, for markets have long provided ample incentive for artists to meet consumers' preferences. And while the state has compelled us to pay for many things we would not have approved if given effective choice, we do not legitimize new error by past error.

Able people have long debated the appropriate purposes of government. But if there are *any* limits to what should concern government, then subsidization of art, however defined and identified, is pushing out the boundaries very far. Indeed, if idiosyncratic behavior not valued by the bulk of the community is to receive largess from the public trough, then little remains of representative government.

Art and Commerce

by Barbara Dodsworth

Today we are aware of the presence of the arts in our society in a broader way than ever before, and we have commerce to thank for it. Business, in response to the desires of consumers, has created reproductions and adaptations of works of fine art that surround us. Few of us are without at least one or two prints of famous works; images from the history of art grace objects of all kinds, down to the workaday tee shirt. The beautiful photography which illustrates commercial art engenders a sensitivity to images in the ordinary observer.

Artists themselves are less than thankful for the presence of the business community in their lives, believing that commerce is a corrupt and discriminatory agent set on repressing free expression. In fact, it works the other way. It is because of business that artists are free to follow their creative muses in any direction they desire. Commerce and the activities of the business community have fostered a higher standard of living and increased leisure time; in short, an atmosphere conducive to the development of all varieties of visual expression, no matter how bizarre. Ultimately this is of benefit to all creators of art. Artists often confuse an inability to make a living in the mode of their choice with the concept of a concerted attempt to repress artistic expression in general. While it is true that only a tiny minority of "fine artists" can support their families with their craft, many more men and women of talent direct their creative energies into extremely productive and lucrative careers in the commercial arts.

Contrary to what most people may think, it was always this way. Artists have always been part of a service industry, creating objects that were part of the daily environment of everyone. From ancient times onward, art has been considered an essential element of life as opposed to a luxury good. There was formerly less of a division between the commercial application of artistic ability and the "fine arts."

Dr. Dodsworth is Director of Seminars at FEE. This article originally appeared in the July 1994 issue of *The Freeman*.

"Fine Art" versus "Commercial Art"

Artists nowadays look down upon those of their ranks who have chosen to work in the commercial arts. This snobbery is ultimately the legacy of the self-promotional efforts of the "divine" Michelangelo, who acted the ultimate prima donna in the creation of his own cult of artist-as-superstar. Somehow artists now think it is a betrayal of one's artistic gifts to use those abilities in the service of the society's needs for the mass application of visual expression. But really this is no different from the fulfillment of a contract specification provided by a patron, just as Pope Julius II hired Michelangelo to decorate his chapel ceiling in a particular way. The result is "fine art" by twentieth-century definitions, but at the time it was hardly different from our modern concept of "commercial art." And one can scarcely deny the creative genius of the painter in his application of his talents to the specific project.

One reason that the modern concept of "fine art" vs. "commercial art" has developed is that the marketing systems that disseminate art are different today than in times past. The museum is a relatively recent phenomenon, and even it itself has changed its relationship to the public in the last twenty years. Art which originally was created to occupy positions in private homes, or to decorate temples and churches, has been removed from its intended setting and placed in a display mode, as if on an altar for worship. The motives of the artist in creating the pieces suddenly took on a different cast; the idea of the piece as product executed for patron for a specific place and purpose has been erased, and instead the work is seen as an expression of the personal vision of the artist.

Working artists blame museums and art galleries for their troubles in making a living, claiming that there are discriminatory practices in the showing of works, that juries of shows are corrupt, and that gallery owners and media critics are in each others' pockets. What is less commonly recognized is that the museum and the gallery system are actually responsible for the success of all artists in general, by raising the social standard of artists to the level of professional; this is in sharp contrast to the Renaissance concept of the artist as artisan (rather like our attitude to, say, plumbers today). By popularizing art in the form of prints, books, postcards, and reproductions, the museum and gallery business have fostered a desire on the part of the public to own art, and even to own original works of art. Surely many artists who do prosper do so because of this heightened awareness.

In addition, the promotion of the "blockbuster exhibition," such as the "Treasures of Tutankhamen" at the Metropolitan Museum of Art in

New York City several years ago, has helped to nurture an awareness of art on the part of the public. The museum's role in this regard is not unlike that of a medieval cathedral, whose exterior, decorated with images of saints and religious stories, would have provided both entertainment and education for the great mass of illiterate peasantry.

Medieval cathedrals, however, differed from modern museums in that they were financed by the Church. The modern museum is funded by a mixture of corporate and private donations with a liberal helping of state monies. Unlike the medieval churchgoer, who paid his share of the church expenses out of his pocket directly, the museum visitor pays for his enjoyment of the art works voluntarily at the time of his actual visit (in discretionary funds) and involuntarily, in amounts which he cannot control, from money he pays the government in the form of taxes. Thus we are all forced to support the activities of public museums, whether we visit them or not.

Changing Modes of Expression

What further separates us from the past is that the modes of expression in previous eras were different from today, and had different functions. In ancient Egypt, for example, art was used as a statist device to propagate religion and state authority; as a result, the visual expression of the Egyptians remained extraordinarily static, changing very little over the course of three thousand years. In Greece, with the development of the concept of democracy and individual freedom, we see a corresponding emphasis in sculpture on the movement of the human body, and a celebration of its beauty and individuality. Art was certainly used for the decoration of temples and for political propaganda, but for the first time we see the beginnings of the concept of consumerism and art: wealthy men were interested in acquiring unique works of art to delight their eye, to enjoy in their own homes. Thus arose the surprisingly modern concept of the glamorous artist, a man who was kissed by divine genius, blessed with extraordinary creative gifts. However, those gifts were used to execute works of art which were specifically created to please the patron, either made to order by contract, or designed with a specific kind of buyer in mind.

Ancient Greece, like the Italian Renaissance, was an abundantly creative period for the arts. One cannot help speculating as to how the political structure fostered these riches. Both periods were marked by an intense feeling of competition between independent city-states, which naturally gave rise to the desire for each to outdo his neighbor in the ornamentation of public buildings and in the level of aesthetic sophistication on the part of the wealthy collector. By contrast, painting and sculpture produced in the Soviet Union were notable for their lack of experimentation, their unimaginative repetition of acceptable visual norms, their low level of creativity and interest. With the emergence of the independent republics, perhaps we will see a flourishing of the visual arts.

On the other hand, since the economic development of the United States has some unnerving parallels with the economic development of the later Roman empire, perhaps we will go the other way. The later years of the Roman empire were marred by the exorbitant increase in taxes, resulting in the erosion of the tax base and the concomitant economic depression. Art work in this period is notable for its increasingly abstract qualities, its lack of devotion to realism, its poor quality, and its reduced abundance. Typical of the period is the pre-made sarcophagus, decorated completely except for a blank medallion all ready to receive the "personalized" portrait of the purchaser, just like a modern headstone. Sound familiar?

Artists are interested in making a living just like everyone else, and will direct their energies into other fields of activity when they observe that the economic climate is not conducive to the production of their craft. It takes only a couple of generations of decline for art to lose its technical virtuosity and become slack and flaccid; no one can draw if no one is available to teach drawing.

But the artists who do make a living out of art—either in the commercial field or in the fine arts—are able to do so because of the receptivity of the environment to aesthetic pleasure. In the promotion of art works through the use of prints and similar items, museums are only developing a concept first introduced hundreds of years ago.

The Rise of the Mass Market

With the Renaissance and the development of printing techniques art was able to take on a new mass market appeal. For the first time, inexpensive woodcuts and engravings of religious themes were available to the individual buyers to take home and enjoy in private. This trend was a reflection of wider currents in social development; in Italy this took the form of what is loosely called "humanism," a cultural movement which sought to secularize Christ and Mary and in the process popularized art. Thanks to the activities of artists like Luca della Robbia, who invented a process to mass produce inexpensive terracotta casts of sculptures, it was suddenly possible for the members of the merchant classes to own works of art comparable in beauty to the masterpieces commissioned by the wealthy. Albrecht Dürer, in Germany, made himself rich by the sale of his exquisite prints; today he is revered for his lovely paintings, but it was his activities in satisfying the mass market demand for art that made his fortune.

Such objects as prints for the medieval and Renaissance public are finally becoming respectable subjects for study by professional art historians, who are fortunately beginning to move away from restricting themselves to the study of masterworks. It is not recognized frequently enough that these "master works" contain only limited creative expression on the part of the artists; such artists were told what to do and how to do it, by the Church or by the specific patron, and were quite circumscribed in their freedom to move beyond those specified limits. By not acknowledging the commercial aspects of what has been regarded as "fine art," a premium has been placed on the creative expression of the individual artist, and a condescending attitude toward commercial art has developed.

Occasionally social currents worked to restrict the development of new trends in artistic expression; typically, since the time of the Greeks, the Western world had always sought out the new and exciting as fashionable. Nevertheless, events like the Black Death in 1347 could conspire with social forces to foster an environment antithetical to the experimental; people of the time believed that the disasters of the mid-fourteenth century were a result of divine punishment for the study of the pre-Christian past, causing the retardataire late Gothic movement in art of the second half of the century. It was as if Giotto, with his vision of the classical past, had never existed; and it was nearly 80 years later that painters finally felt free to express their admiration for Roman sculpture, and the Renaissance was born.

But even during the Renaissance those works that we acknowledge to be the creations of pure genius were actually charged with commercial implications and designed with business in mind. Art flourishes most dramatically when it pairs creativity with business acumen; artistic success should be measured not only by the beauty of the work, but by how well it demonstrates a response to the specifics of its creation.

In Praise of Billboards

by Lawrence Person

I recently took a car trip from central Texas to northern Virginia. Though my journey was of an entirely practical nature (two straight days of driving, with no time for sightseeing), it gave me a new appreciation for something I had not really given much thought to: billboards. Despite the scathing criticism heaped upon them for aesthetic reasons, billboards are actually possessed of a number of unsung virtues.

First of all, billboards are a valuable source of information, especially when you're making a long trip through an unfamiliar area. If it's getting near lunchtime, and I see a sign that says "McArches—30 miles," then I have more information on how and when to plan my stops. Likewise, if I am starting to run low on gas, a sign for Texxon might tell me not only how far ahead the station is, but whether it has a mechanic on duty, the best way to get there, and so forth. Finally, if I'm starting to get sleepy, a billboard can tell me how far to the next motel, and what it might be charging for a room. As a consumer, every piece of information I have helps me make better choices.

Some states have a government substitute for billboards: signs with little metal plates bearing the establishment's logo, distance-to information, and which exit to take. Like most state-owned substitutes, their usefulness falls far short of the real thing. For one thing, these little signs don't tell you the prices of a room for the night, a gallon of unleaded, or a large order of fries. For another, they don't give you all the other information a business might provide on their billboard: *Homebaked Cookies! Air Conditioning! A Toledo Mudhens Collector's Glass with Every Purchase!*

Despite these many virtues, you almost never hear a kindly word for billboards. Critics charge they're "sight pollution," as though they emit cancer-causing agents that infect the body via the optic nerve. These same critics go on to charge that billboards clutter up the natural landscape, and, above all, are inferior to trees.

The poet Ogden Nash wrote:

Mr. Person is former editor of *Citizens Agenda*. This article originally appeared in the September 1993 issue of *The Freeman*.

I think that I shall never see
A billboard lovely as a tree.
Indeed, unless the billboards fall
I'll never see a tree at all.

Fair enough. Such critics are, after all, entitled to their opinion. There are a lot of things I might personally label "sight pollution," including those hideous modern art sculptures that seem to spring up like giant metal weeds in front of every government building. Indeed, between the two I much prefer billboards, especially since they weren't constructed using my tax dollars. However, there is a big difference between saying something is ugly and saying that it should be regulated or outlawed.

As far as cluttering up the natural landscape goes, there are a lot of things that do that, including houses, cars, highways, and people, but you don't see special-interest groups trying to legislate *them* out of existence. (OK, a few environmentalists *are* trying to outlaw all of the above, including people. However, since people make up the vast majority of the voting population, they haven't made much progress on this front.) I must admit that I, too, think that the average tree is more attractive than the average billboard. Then again, a tree never told me that I could get three Supertacos for 99 cents either. Also, if my trip is any indication, trees are in no danger of disappearing anytime soon. On the way up they outnumbered billboards at least 10,000 to 1.

Aesthetic differences aside, it shouldn't matter whether a billboard is beautiful or ugly: Both are protected by the right of private property. The idea that someone's property rights should be taken away because a handful (or even a majority) of people deem a particular structure "ugly" is absurd.

There is a particularly insidious line of reasoning being marshaled by anti-billboard forces these days. "Because billboards are profitable only because they are placed along major public thoroughfares," goes this argument, "the right of private property does not apply, and thus it is well within a government's right to regulate them out of existence." The implications of such reasoning are truly frightening. This same logic applies to every single business that operates along any public road, and since the overwhelming majority of roads in the United States are government controlled, the scale of government intervention permissible under such a doctrine is staggering.

Indeed, as long as we're going to have the government enforce aesthetic dictates, it is only a small step from regulating the billboards along a road to regulating the cars on it. In the future, we can expect to see the Good Taste Police handing out tickets to those wretched miscreants whose cars need body work or a new paint job. The scourge of automotive sight pollution *must* be driven off our streets, which means no more purple Cadillacs, custom low-riders, jacked-up pickup trucks, or any other vehicle that fails to conform with the New Government Aesthetics Standards.

In addition to property rights, billboards are also protected by another of our basic freedoms: the right to free speech. In Austin, Texas, there used to be a mural billboard that proclaimed: FREE NELSON MANDELA! While this is an overtly political message, commercial messages on billboards are also expressions of that same right to free speech. The First Amendment makes no distinction between commercial and non-commercial speech, and the message "Two McBurgers—$1.99" should be no less constitutionally protected than "Free Nelson Mandela."

Finally, billboards can be a source of humor. While driving in Tennessee, I saw a billboard for one particular establishment proudly proclaim: FOOD * GAS * ELVIS COLLECTIBLES. Now there's one thing *no* government sign is *ever* going to tell me!

Kosher Cops

by Jacob Sullum

When presented with packaged food, my 5-year-old niece will carefully examine the wrapper, box, or label, looking for the symbol that assures her it's OK to eat: a *U* inside a circle, which certifies that the food has been prepared according to Jewish dietary laws, under the supervision of the Union of Orthodox Jewish Congregations of America. She will not accept a mere *K*, which represents the manufacturer's unverified statement that the product is kosher.

You might think that if a preschooler is capable of making such distinctions, so is the average adult, observant Jew. But some people don't want to take any chances. For decades regulators in 20 states have inspected businesses selling ostensibly kosher food to make sure they follow the laws of *kashrut*—which, among other things, forbid certain categories of food, require the separation of meat and milk, and specify procedures for slaughtering and preparing meat.

State *kashrut* supervision has recently come under attack in the courts. Last year the New Jersey Supreme Court overturned that state's *kashrut* regulations as an unconstitutional establishment of religion. In Maryland, a hot-dog vendor has brought a similar challenge against a Baltimore ordinance, and the case is pending in federal court.

Both cases hinge on subtle and complicated analyses of what constitutes a secular legislative purpose, an advancement of religion, or an excessive entanglement with religion. But they also raise a question that the courts have not been asked to decide: Is there any area at all where consumers can be expected to look out for their own interests? State intervention in the kosher-food market illustrates a regulatory mindset that has become disturbingly common in the United States. This mindset insists that barbers must be licensed to protect consumers from bad haircuts; that every bottle of beer, wine, and liquor must alert drinkers that "consumption of alcoholic beverages impairs your ability to drive a car or operate machinery"; and that food companies must not be allowed to announce that their products contain "no cholesterol,"

Mr. Sullum is a former editor of *Reason* magazine. The article originally appeared in the July 1993 issue of *The Freeman*.

lest consumers be misled into believing that a diet consisting exclusively of margarine and vegetable oil is healthy.

While the absurdity of these measures may be readily apparent, state *kashrut* supervision is less obviously unnecessary. After all, when a merchant or restauranteur represents that a produce or meal is kosher, he is making an assertion that may be crucially important to the buyer. Moreover, the assertion cannot be readily verified by examining the food itself. Chicken that has been slaughtered according to Jewish law is indistinguishable from ordinary chicken. A cake that has been baked with vegetable shortening looks the same as a cake that has been baked with lard. Yet kosher food (especially meat) often commands a higher price than non-kosher food. Like a jeweler who convinces customers that his fake diamonds are the real thing, a business that could get away with passing non-kosher food off as kosher would stand to make a tidy profit.

Indeed, defenders of state *kashrut* supervision have argued that it is simply a way of enforcing laws against consumer fraud. For example, Nathan Lewin, an attorney with the National Jewish Commission on Law and Public Affairs, told *The Washington Post*: "If the state doesn't regulate, consumers will have no assurance that a food is really kosher. . . . Consumers may be at the mercy of unscrupulous vendors who will sell non-kosher food as kosher. Someone who cares so little about the laws of *kashrut* could sell a product that contains pork and say it's kosher, and there will be no one around to stop that."

Even if you know next to nothing about kosher food, you might wonder how observant Jews managed to get by for thousands of years without the assistance of agencies such as New Jersey's Bureau of Kosher Enforcement. And if you're familiar with the dining and shopping habits of Jews who keep kosher, you will recognize that Lewin, like the "unscrupulous vendors" he describes, is guilty of misrepresentation. He neglects to mention that the very conditions that invite fraud in the kosher-food industry have led to an elaborate private system of consumer protection.

Private *Kashrut* Supervision

As my niece could tell you, Jews rely upon certification by religious authorities to determine whether something is kosher. There are more than 100 *kashrut* supervision services worldwide, plus publications, such as *Kashrus Magazine*, devoted to covering developments that might concern a Jew who observes the dietary laws. In addition to organizations such as the Orthodox Union, individuals often serve as *kashrut* supervisors, or *mashgichim*. (These are often rabbis, but they need not be; anyone with the proper training can do the job.)

In Los Angeles, where I live, two local organizations and several independent *mashgichim* certify bakeries, butcher shops, and restaurants. Supervision generally involves a full-time employee trained in the laws of *kashrut*, supplemented by outside inspectors who make surprise visits on a regular basis. If you want to know whether a business has supervision, you can ask to see its certificate, which is usually on display.

Obviously, this system works only if consumers can safely assume that such certificates are genuine. As the New Jersey Supreme Court observed: "Just as the State may bar promotion of products as having been tested by a certain testing laboratory when they have not been so tested, and just as the State may bar promotion of products as having been endorsed by a certain consumer magazine when they have not been so endorsed, so may the State bar promotion of products as having been prepared under the supervision of a particular rabbi or group of rabbis when they have not been so prepared." Protecting citizens from such fraud is a legitimate function of the state.

Even with a prohibition on fraud, the system of private supervision is not perfect. It relies, to a considerable degree, on trust. Consumers trust the *mashgichim*, and the *mashgichim*, to some extent, trust business owners. This trust is based largely on shared religious values. But both *mashgichim* and the businesses they supervise have to worry about maintaining their reputations in the face of competition, which is not true of state inspectors. An establishment that has been known to mislead its customers will not stay in business long, and a *mashgiach* who is known for corruption or carelessness can no longer practice his occupation.

At first glance, the New Jersey and Maryland cases seem to suggest a need for state supervision. In the New Jersey case, a rabbi working for the state cited Ran-Dav's County Kosher in Roseland for several violations of *kashrut* rules, including failure to devein calves' tongues and storage of non-kosher chicken in the same freezer with kosher chicken. But County Kosher is also under the private supervision of another Orthodox rabbi, who insists that the state inspector is mistaken. Rather than a case of fraud that would have gone undetected without state regulation, this seems to be a case of honest disagreement between two *mashgichim*. In the final analysis, the consumer must decide whether County Kosher's supervisor can be trusted. This is the kind of decision that observant Jews must make all the time, often after consulting with their own rabbis (who may in turn ask an organization such as the Orthodox Union).

In the Maryland case, a rabbi from Baltimore's Bureau of Kosher Food and Meat Control cited hot-dog vendor George Barghout for selling kosher frankfurters after cooking them on the same rotisserie as non-kosher frankfurters. Yet if this was his practice Barghout could not possibly have obtained a certificate of *kashrut* from a reputable *mashgiach*. Passers-by who were serious about keeping kosher would not have taken the vendor's word that the hot dogs were kosher; they would have insisted upon verification. In this case and in general, government *kashrut* supervision protects only the lenient or lackadaisical.

The Washington Post reported that the New Jersey Supreme Court's decision "may mean consumers determined to keep kosher may have to do a lot more homework themselves on the products they buy." In fact, observant Jews in New Jersey and elsewhere will continue to do what they have always done: look for the mark or certificate showing that a product or establishment passes muster with a religious authority they trust. This is really not a major obstacle, especially since kosher-food consumers tend to be highly motivated.

A Special-Interest Plea

In the end, the arguments for state *kashrut* supervision boil down to a special-interest plea: Some kosher-food consumers would like the government to subsidize their search and transaction costs. They may feel that the added assurance of state regulation allows them to be a little less careful. Or they may simply get a psychological benefit from knowing that private *mashgichim* are backed up by government inspectors. "I would want the support of the state," says Rabbi Nissim Davidi, administrator of *kashrut* supervision with the Rabbinical Council of California. At the same time, he admits that he's never had any contact with California's kosher-food regulators, and he's not sure exactly what they do.

You might think that state *kashrut* supervision would long ago have attracted the attention of anti-Semites. But the ACLU, anxious to maintain the separation of church and state, seems to worry about it a lot more than the American Nazi Party does. On the other hand, anti-Semitic propaganda has for years railed against what hate groups call "the kosher tax." This is the alleged increase in price that results when a food company pays for private *kashrut* supervision, so that its products can display a mark of certification. According to the hate literature, the Jews are mysteriously able to impose this price hike on manufacturers and consumers. For those who don't buy Jewish-conspiracy theories, a more plausible explanation is that the companies have calculated that the extra business generated by *kashrut* certification more than makes up for the cost of supervision. (Hence no price increase is necessary.)

Ironically, it's this private, voluntary, market-driven process that attracts the attention of anti-Semites. So far, they seem oblivious to state *kashrut* supervision, which actually is a public subsidy, albeit a drop in the ocean of special-interest benefits doled out by government. I won't tell them if you won't.

Telecompetition: The Free Market Road to the Information Highway: A Review

by Raymond J. Keating

Technological change has pushed the telecommunications-information industry into a dramatic and exciting phase of development. Information has always been a most valuable commodity, and now the means of storing, moving, and manipulating it are advancing rapidly while costs plummet.

In turn, such developments are altering the world economy. The globe is shrinking as international competition intensifies. Rather than ensuring the ascendence of large multinational corporations or enhancement of government controls, as many have feared, the revolution in telecommunications and computers has empowered individuals and increased the mobility of capital. Both economic competition and the ability of labor and capital to avoid, for example, severe taxation and regulation are enhanced.

Ironically, however, just as technological developments are strengthening the power and productivity of the individual, the question dominating current public policy debate is the extent of state's role in the telecommunications market. Should we be centrally planning a government-led telecommunications industrial policy, or turning to a competition-based, market-driven telecommunications industry? Persuasively weighing in on the side of deregulation and freer markets is Lawrence Gasman with his book *Telecompetition* (Cato Institute, 1994).

Gasman makes a compelling case for how the convergence of industries and enhanced competition not only support, but necessitate the deregulation of telecommunications. Of course, deregulation also is called for due to the plodding nature of government, which remains a severe roadblock to expanding the reach of new technologies. In fact, Gasman declares: "The general ignorance of technological developments displayed by those who regulate the telecommunications industry is appalling. It also indicates why one cannot expect too much from the government when it comes to a successful industrial policy for the

---

Mr. Keating is chief economist with the Small Business Survival Foundation. This article originally appeared in the November 1994 issue of *The Freeman*.

telecommunications industry." Another reason for low expectations is governmental ignorance of how markets work.

Telecommunications advancements are blurring the lines drawn by regulators who try to neatly separate industries. The author notes the fluid nature of information format and storage: "Once it is digitized, voice video, text, and data are all much the same. . . . [N]ew forms of multimedia communications are emerging in which text, voice, and image communications are combined in a single interactive, user-friendly format." Gasman continues: "It is this fluidity of information formats that constitutes convergence. Convergence has resulted from both the recognition that all information can be converted into the same binary digital form and the development of micro-electronics that makes such a conversion possible while providing the means for conveniently and economically manipulating digital information. Convergence is not only central to the Information Age, it affects every level of information technology—hardware, software, and services."

Gasman masterfully illustrates how convergence seriously undermines the government's rationale for extensive telecommunications regulation. For example, he argues that in light of alternative-access carriers and local wireless communications, it is becoming increasingly difficult to legitimately refer to a "local telephone monopoly." In this era, in fact, the source of any true monopoly power emanates from the government. Gasman observes the detrimental effects of an exclusive government franchise: "The existence of communications monopolies slows the introduction of new and innovative services by the industry. The cable-telco dispute is just one example of how government-created monopolies and misguided antitrust action can delay new services."

The author predicts that absent government interference, for example, "an eclectic industry structure for local video distribution might well grow up, designed to fit the needs of local markets. In some areas, telephone companies would supply both the video programming and the channels through which that programming is carried. In others, cable companies would supply programming through the telephone-company networks. . . . In a few areas we might see cable companies upgrade their own networks with switching gear to enable them to offer the kinds of advanced voice and video services that seem today to be the sole province of telephone companies."

Gasman argues for allowing local telephone companies to enter any local, regional, national, or international business they choose—"inside or outside the telecommunications field." Likewise, "any company financially and technically capable of offering local telephone service should be free to do so."

Gasman also makes a compelling case for a pure property-rights system regarding the broadcast spectrum, rather than the current government allocation and temporary licensing system. In lieu of suffering through government delays and politicization, "if spectrum allocation were left to market forces, the providers of new services would bid directly for the spectrum owned by existing users." Gasman draws a straight-forward analogy: "Just as landowners are given title to a particular piece of real estate, spectrum owners would receive a title, allowing them to transmit at certain frequencies with specified powers from given locations. And just as landowners can buy and sell properties, spectrum owners would be allowed to buy and sell their transmission rights. The result would no doubt be speedier deployment of new services responding to consumer rather than government interests." Again, the plodding hand of government must be replaced by the dynamics of the marketplace.

Proponents of a government information infrastructure also are refuted in *Telecompetition*. Instead of taking the telecommunications infrastructure on another trip down the misdirected path of industrial policy, Gasman sagaciously concludes: "Eventually private initiative will undoubtedly produce a network offering all the broadcast services infrastructuralists are so eager to produce with taxpayers' dollars. The difference is that private companies will be certain to produce services businesses and consumers want to buy."

As the author notes, much of telecommunications regulation springs from the economist's use of the perfect competition model. A perfectly competitive market where all companies are price takers and offer homogeneous products is an economic fairy tale. Unfortunately, it also can be turned into economic nightmare when wielded by government officials who seek to regulate when a market fails the perfect competition test. To the contrary, a dynamic, entrepreneurial economy will be flush with temporary monopolies—a result of creation, innovation, and competition. This should nowhere be more evident than in the telecommunications industry. If government establishes and protects property rights, and then largely gets out of the way, as Lawrence Gasman suggests, consumers and the economy will reap great rewards.

Telecompetition is a highly readable primer on the often complex subject of telecommunications public policy. One can only hope that such market-oriented writers as Gasman, along with George Gilder and Peter Huber, prevail in the government-vs.-the-market struggle in telecommunications.

Regulation of Telecommunications

by Clint Bolick

America has produced many revolutions in its first 220 years, but perhaps none since its founding embodies such enormous potential for shaping our global destiny as the telecommunications revolution.

Cable television and related technologies have thrust us to the threshold of an information age, brimming with potential for increased freedom. From our individual homes we can direct more of our own affairs, utilizing vastly more sophisticated yet personalized information exchange mechanisms that make possible voluntary contact with anyone with whom we wish to communicate.

That this amazing 20th-century revolution could occur at all is a tribute to the American Revolution of 1776, whose leaders charted a unique commitment to a "free marketplace of ideas," enshrined in the First Amendment to the Constitution. This commitment fostered a society characterized by an unprecedented open and robust exchange of views, as well as an unquenchable thirst for new technologies to facilitate that exchange.

The telecommunications revolution is the product of free, creative minds and an unfettered communications marketplace. But as we enter the era in which electronic media will displace print as the dominant vehicle for communications, we face the same decision that confronted the founders of the American experiment: we must choose between the market and the state to regulate the commerce of ideas. Our decision, like that of the founders, will determine whether the technologies of our day will usher in an era of human freedom—or will operate to subvert that freedom.

The Telecommunications Revolution

What is this revolution that is taking place around us? What are the opportunities that it presents?

Some of the new technologies are already here, dramatically expanding the horizons of information exchange. At the forefront is

Mr. Bolick is Vice President and Director of Litigation at the Institute for Justice. This article originally appeared in the September 1984 issue of *The Freeman*.

cable television, which utilizes coaxial cables to bring subscribers a wide variety of programming alternatives. Typical cable systems expand viewer choices exponentially, offering local origination and satellite transmission as well as distant broadcast programming. Virtually infinite channel capacity can accommodate the most specialized entertainment, news, educational, community affairs, cultural, political, and commercial programming. Already there are 35 million cable subscribers in the United States alone, and by 1990 the percentage of television households patronizing cable services will grow from the present 35 percent to 62 percent. Subscription levels in Western Europe are rising rapidly as well.

Alternative technologies promise stiff competition for these services. Direct broadcast satellites (DBS) bypass cable by transmitting signals directly to dishes installed on subscribers' property. Multi-point distribution service (MDS) transmits video services to individual subscribers via microwaves. Pay television uses broadcast signals that are "unscrambled" at the customer's residence.

The accelerating development of computers, two-way "interactive" services, and fiber optics will further expand the ability of individuals to obtain information from diverse sources and to communicate with one another. From private homes and businesses, we may now access computer data banks and share information with others. "Electronic newspapers," combining traditional publishing with satellite transmission, have enhanced the development of national media and can provide the latest information specifically tailored to suit personal needs and demands. Home banking and a host of other home consumer services are available. And the advent of instantaneous voting via cable can potentially transform a large nation into a town hall-style democracy. As Ralph Lee Smith concluded more than a decade ago in *The Wired Nation*, "In short, every home and office can obtain a communications center of a breadth and flexibility to influence every aspect of private and community life."

The Role of Government

The extent to which these prospects are realized will largely depend on the role of government. All of the new technologies have been subjected to varying levels of regulation. In the United States, for example, heavy regulation by the Federal Communications Commission (FCC) throttled cable television's development for several years. Subsequently, however, the FCC reversed its course and deregulated cable, immediately leading to accelerated technological developments that restored America's leadership role in the telecommunications revolution.

In Europe, governmental control over new technologies has slowed progress and delayed service. Former West German Chancellor Helmut Schmidt stalled cable television progress during his tenure, chastising it as "more dangerous than nuclear power," and refusing to countenance cable development in that country. Now, many European nations, aware at last of cable's potential and aghast at America's invasion of their home turfs through that medium, are anxiously playing catch-up.

Why is America the leader in the communications revolution? In large part, it is because of its predilection toward free market solutions and its faith in technology, while Europe tends toward greater state involvement in the economy. What makes America truly unique, however, is that the free communications marketplace is not simply an economic policy, but a matter of constitutional doctrine as well. The First Amendment has fostered not only freedom of speech, but also the virtual explosion of technology that has made that precious freedom more meaningful than ever.

Whether the new technologies will ultimately be used to expand or restrict prospects for freedom, however, is still an open question. The information age may witness an expansion of individual sovereignty as never before—or a loss of that sovereignty to state control. In each of the modern industrial nations, the time for decision-making is at hand. As Ithiel de Sola Pool concludes in *Technologies of Freedom*,

> The problem is worldwide. . . . The onus is on us to determine whether free societies in the twenty-first century will conduct electronic communications under the conditions of freedom established . . . through centuries of struggle, or whether that great achievement will become lost.

Choices and Consequences

In choosing the mechanism that will regulate the telecommunications revolution, two polar opposites are possible: the nightmarish world of George Orwell's *1984* in which all communications are controlled by the state, and an unfettered marketplace of ideas in which a free press thrives.

The first alternative is vividly depicted by Orwell as a world utterly devoid of freedom. Orwell recognized that a totalitarian state could be achieved and maintained only through absolute control over ideas and communications. The state created a language, "Newspeak," with which it could control the scope of ideas and rewrite history under the aegis of the Ministry of Truth. It utilized a highly sophisticated technology capable of monitoring all personal thoughts and communications. Orwell traced the development of this awesome power:

> The invention of print . . . made it easier to manipulate public opinion, and the film and the radio carried the process further. With the development of television, and the technical advance which it made possible . . . [t]he possibility of enforcing not only complete obedience to the will of the state, but complete uniformity of opinion on all subjects, now existed for the first time.

In Orwell's society, the state controls all information dissemination and proscribes all contrary thoughts. The submission of the citizenry is ensured by the Thought Police, who carefully monitor all communications through two-way telecommunications devices designed to serve the needs of the state:

> The instrument (the telescreen, it was called) could be dimmed, but there was no way of shutting it off completely. . . . The telescreen received and transmitted simultaneously. . . . You had to live—did live, from habit that became instinct—in the assumption that every sound you made was overheard.

The world of *1984* is a dismal one, a world in which the new technologies are subverted to constrict, rather than expand, voluntary interpersonal communications. Orwell's message is replete with tacit warnings against permitting government to control the exchange of ideas and the mechanisms that facilitate that exchange. The technology of *1984* exists today—as does the potential for tyrannous governments to exploit it to subvert freedom.

Another course is possible. In stark contrast to *1984* is the historical experience of the press in the United States. The American founders well understood the dangers of vesting in government the power to suppress and censor speech. They recognized in the Virginia Declaration of Rights in 1776 that "the freedom of the press is one of the greatest bulwarks of liberty, and can never be restrained except by despotick [sic] governments."

Freedom of Speech

Fresh from their experience with the suppression of colonial speech under the rule of the British crown, many of the founders refused to support the new Constitution until freedom of speech was ensured. Resisting the opportunity to seize such power for themselves, they instead incorporated into their basic law the First Amendment: "Congress shall make no law. . . abridging the freedom of speech, or of the press." As Justice Hugo Black observed almost two centuries later, it was established for the first time that "[t]he press was to serve the governed, not the governors."

Ever since the acquittal of publisher John Peter Zenger of charges of seditious libel in 1735, the press in America has been immunized from government interference far more than any other enterprise. Rather than relying on the state to protect the public from "dangerous" or false ideas, the First Amendment vests that right and responsibility in the citizens themselves. As Thomas Jefferson explained, it is "better to trust the public judgment, rather than the magistrate. . . . And hitherto the public has performed that office with wonderful correctness."

The founders correctly believed that the only dependable and enduring safeguard for the free marketplace of ideas was to bar the government from exercising editorial control over private communications. As Justice Potter Stewart explained, the First Amendment "is a clear command that government must never be allowed to lay its heavy editorial hand on any newspaper in this country." The concept of free speech has been applied to protect the commerce of ideas between willing communicators, and those willing to receive such communications. The Supreme Court has generally recognized that any departure from these protections would have serious adverse consequences. As Justice Thurgood Marshall observed, "Our whole constitutional heritage rebels at the thought of giving government the power to control men's minds."

The results of the commitment to free speech and a free press are readily apparent in the vigorous exchange of ideas which is a hallmark of American society. Anyone with a typewriter, telephone, or soapbox may freely transmit views to those wishing to receive them. These constitutional guarantees protect dissenting viewpoints and provide mighty deterrents against government tyranny. Indeed, but for the First Amendment, the horror of *1984* could be today's reality.

The Market or the State?

The idea of a free communications marketplace essentially unregulated by the state was a radical one in 1776, and sadly enough remains so today. Particularly with the onset of new technologies, many today advocate some form of "mixed" state and private control of speech, for any of a number of high-sounding reasons. But as Ludwig von Mises warned, the issue is always the same—"the market or the state; and there is no third solution."

Those who advocate mixed control have concluded that individuals should relinquish some measure of their sovereignty for the greater good. All of their rationalizations rest on the notion that the state enjoys a superior capability to determine the interests of society as a whole in the information age.

The first of these justifications is the most transparent. Many government officials view regulation as a vital safeguard against "commercial exploitation" of consumers. This paternalistic notion seeks to justify imposed choices by government while proscribing the individual autonomy provided by the market. But far from exploiting consumers, the market inherently provides the most effective consumer-protection mechanism possible—competition. Due to omnipresent pressures in the market for technological change, the new media must be fiercely competitive. Those entrepreneurs offering the finest products, lowest prices, most personalized services, and latest technical advances will prosper. Conversely, government interference inevitably adds regulatory costs and hampers profitability, thus dampening innovation and choice.

A second justification is fiscal policy. The revenues certain to be realized from the telecommunications revolution are tempting to cash-poor governmental entities. Further, harnessing these new technologies could provide the cornerstone for revived "industrial policy" in many countries. This modern-day mercantilism suffers, however, from the same fundamental flaw that plagues all state-controlled industries: the gains to society's wealth obtained by state displacement of or interference with private enterprise pale in long-term comparison with free industries, which enjoy greater incentive to maximize efficiency, productivity, and improvement. Indeed, those governments which have restrained the new communications technologies are in a virtual frenzy over the spectacle of massive consumer spending in their own countries for the goods and services made possible by these technologies in less-regulated countries. Many have commenced policies of protectionism and government subsidies in a belated and futile attempt to steer consumers away from products they desire.

A third rationale for government regulation is "scarcity" of one sort or another. This is the justification typically cited by those wishing to impose content control to protect the public interest. One type is physical scarcity, which holds that airwaves are limited and thus may only be fairly allocated and regulated by the state. The physical scarcity concept brought about a major departure from First Amendment protections as communications exchange shifted from the press to broadcast media. While newspapers continued to receive full protection, television programmers were subjected to substantial "public interest" regulation, much of which was upheld in the courts. The result has been stifling homogenization in programming as producers concentrate as much on satisfying governmental dictates as they do on customer demands. Still another result, however, has been the rapid development of the new alternative technologies, which offer increasingly stiff competition to the broadcast media. If it was ever a valid premise for government regulation, the physical scarcity rationale is clearly rendered obsolete by the new competitors and the unlimited programming options they present.

A second form of scarcity is "economic scarcity," or the theory of "natural monopoly." Some theorists argue that many communications technologies require such intensive capital investments that only one producer may profitably serve a given market. Ostensibly protecting the citizenry from "monopoly power," the governmental entity chooses and licenses a single producer as a "franchisee" or "common carrier," and then subjects that producer to extensive taxation and regulatory control. This notion dates at least as far back as 1585, when the British crown awarded monopoly privileges to publishing guilds. The artificial restriction on the number of publishers facilitated government censorship, but was ultimately undermined by sustained illicit competition.

"Economic Scarcity"

In America, the concept of economic scarcity was suggested as a rationale for requiring newspapers to publish replies to unfavorable reporting—an argument the Supreme Court firmly rejected. But although the Court has opposed even the most "benign" regulation of newspaper content, it has yet to fully extend this protection to the new media. It has failed to do so because it asserts that differences in the characteristics of new media justify different degrees of First Amendment protection.

This approach contradicts the teachings of America's founders. They did not provide protection only to the press, but to speech itself as well, perhaps anticipating that new mechanisms would arise to challenge the press as the prime facilitator of communications exchange. Speech is no less an exchange of ideas if it is transmitted by television, cable, or satellite rather than by newspapers. Yet the courts have departed from First Amendment principles and allowed state regulation of radio and television, and now face a similar decision in the context of cable and other new media. Any further failure to zealously protect the free communications marketplace portends distressing consequences.

The American Cable Experience

Nowhere is the abandonment of First Amendment values more apparent than in the cable television arena. Despite deregulation at the federal level, regulation of cable in America is increasingly extensive, restraining the full realization of that medium's enormous potential and laying the groundwork for massive state interference with editorial processes traditionally entrusted to private discretion.

With the lifting of most regulations at the federal level in the last decade, municipal governments have made cable television a focus of attention. Relying on all three justifications—public interest, revenue, and economic scarcity—they have subjected cable to broader regulation than any communications medium in American history.

Starting with the premise that cable television is a "natural monopoly," municipalities award exclusive franchises, in effect rendering economic scarcity a self-fulfilling prophecy. Based on its control of the public streets, the governmental entity essentially precludes other firms from entering the community. In return, it exacts enormous tribute from the winner of the franchise. Typical concessions include expensive franchise fees, "public access" studios, subsidized programming for special interest groups, and review of program content. While filling public coffers and placing the strong arm of government on the pulse of local communications, these regulations add nearly 25 percent to the cost of cable programming and limit subscribers to a single choice for cable services.

Unsound Reasoning

The rationales for government control in the cable context are fundamentally unsound. Cable is an *unnatural* monopoly; few companies compete head-to-head only because the system of local franchises and pervasive regulations makes it unprofitable and frequently illegal to do so. Even without direct competition, however, the existence of alternative technologies provides the important disciplinary effects of the marketplace, making "public interest" regulation wholly unnecessary. Open entry policies and the constant threat of competition would accomplish the same end. Indeed, some local governments, recognizing that the natural monopoly myth rests on tenuous assumptions, have acted to exclude from their communities not only additional cable companies but competing alternative technologies as well.

If the First Amendment is displaced and government control over cable is entrenched, the state will be free to further invade the sanctity of the communications marketplace. At least one franchise requires the installation of devices for empowering government officials, at any hour of the day or night, to turn on every subscriber's television set and broadcast "emergency" messages. Two-way telecommunications capacity—a central feature of Orwell's scenario—renders the specter of government control even more alarming.

The courts have yet to definitively rule on the First Amendment implications of government control over cable, and the battle over these issues will be a long and fierce one. While much of the upcoming legal fight may center on economic questions, the basic issue is a moral one: should individuals be autonomous in choosing what, how, and to whom to communicate, or should those choices be made by government? The resolution of this vital question will loom large in determining the future of human freedom.

The Challenge Ahead

America is unique in its commitment to an uninhibited marketplace of ideas. Yet America itself is precipitously close to discarding that commitment, which for more than 200 years has supported its claim to moral leadership in the area of freedom of speech.

Even before the rapid development of the new media, Justice William O. Douglas warned of the dangers involved in abandoning the commitment to First Amendment principles on the basis of technological change:

The struggle for liberty has been a struggle against government. . . . [I]t is anathema to the First Amendment to allow government any role of censorship over newspapers, magazines, books, art, music, TV, radio or any other aspect of the press. . . . My conclusion is that the TV and radio stand in the same protected position as do newspapers and magazines . . . for the fear that Madison and Jefferson had of government intrusions is perhaps even more relevant to TV and radio than it is to other like publications.

With the onset of cable and related technologies, the stakes are higher still. We are on the brink of facilitating voluntary communications and commerce on a scale unprecedented in history. Whether the telecommunications revolution will be a tool for freedom or for suppression depends upon the policy choices we make today. As de Sola Pool warns, "It would be dire if the laws we make today . . . in such an information society were subversive of its freedom."

If we are to avoid the prophecies of totalitarian doom, we must resolve to protect the legacy of freedom which we have inherited, and to expand it to the worldwide scale now made more possible than ever by the new technologies.

III. A CARING SOCIETY:
HEALTH, EDUCATION, AND WELFARE
WITHOUT COERCION

Home Schooling: A Personal Experience

by Hannah Lapp

"Where did you get your education?" or "Which college do you attend?" are questions I find harder to answer than most people do. Education has meant much more to me than mere academic study.

My own formal education, and that of most of my 11 brothers and sisters, consisted of eight years of schooling at home. Our teacher was Mother, or our big sister Lydia. Going to school meant going to an upstairs hall or other suitable room in one of the sundry and fascinating dwellings we called home in those days. Our curriculum contained the basics for each grade in English, arithmetic, geography, and so on. Lydia selected our books from companies such as Scott, Foresman and Company, Laidlaw Brothers, and other publishers; some of the texts were as old as the McGuffey Readers.

As students, we were aware that education is serious business, and we worked our brains to the fullest. School was a thrilling opportunity. It opened the doors of knowledge and was a path into the mysteries of grown-up life.

Inborn in a healthy child is a thirst for the liberating powers of knowledge. Our teacher utilized these instincts of her students in introducing us not only to hard academic facts, but to an infinite learning process whose boundaries only our own self-discipline could shape. School learning meant learning how to expend mental energy to get information we wanted. Thus our minds were exercised not only in academic questions, but also in such difficult social concepts as freedom through meeting obligations, and the price of privileges.

"How can eight years be enough?" is a justifiable challenge offered against an educational background such as my own. Certainly the potential of young minds is much too valuable to justify halting education at age 14.

It does not occur to me to separate the education I received after the age of 14 from my eight years of formal schooling. For I regard the disciplined acquisition of knowledge too highly to draw its boundaries at the doors of an academic institution. I also respect it too much to

---

Ms. Lapp is a dairy farmer and writer in Cassadaga, New York. This article originally appeared in the April 1991 issue of *The Freeman*.

assume that it is best taken care of by a government bureaucracy or any other monopolizing agency. For where, but within individual minds and circumstances, can it be determined what type of knowledge is the most needful and how it is best obtained?

The most suitable continued education for me and most of my siblings involved such things as skills training on our farm and self-help through reading, using libraries, taking short courses in specific subjects, and so on. Those of us who later decided to pursue specialized professions had no problem passing a high school equivalency test and taking off from there.

Even during my years of going to school at home, those hours of book-learning that qualified as a legal education were only a small part of my total education. More than we could fully comprehend at the time, we youngsters were receiving daily moral, emotional, and intellectual exercises that were just as important in preparing us for adult life as the mandatory hours spent in school. For just as becoming literate was essential to a self-sufficient and productive future, so also was learning responsibility and proper human coexistence. These concepts were instilled in us through necessity in our large, close family with many children to feed.

My family's search for a suitable private school, and finally the search for a region having laws compatible with home schooling, was a major factor in our many migrations when I was small. It was also a factor in our often tight finances. We children learned thriftiness from infancy, and enjoyed few niceties. But it was enough for us to be healthy and happy.

The same circumstances that appeared at times unfortunate endowed us with learning experiences which could well be envied by the less needy.

For example, my older brothers and sisters were compelled to search out employment from a young age in order to help support the family. During one school term, two of my sisters took turns babysitting for a neighbor lady who was consequently able to stay off public assistance by holding a job. In the absence of welfare, two low-income families were drawn together to trade resources, thus benefiting all parties involved. My sisters were able to maintain their grades in school by taking their books to work, and their job in itself provided excellent hands-on education. Lydia, one of the two, would go on to instruct her younger siblings and, afterward, many other students during her teaching career.

Our quest for jobs where we could work together to support ourselves while being home schooled led us to a number of different states.

Among other ventures, we traveled about in our family station wagon, following fruit harvests in their season. Where our employers permitted it, family members six years old and up helped to earn. It was through their children's ambitious participation that my parents were able to save up a considerable sum of money so that by 1972 they purchased the farmstead that would come to embody our long-time aspirations.

Dad picked Chautauqua County in western New York for the site of our farm because of reasonable land prices and job opportunities on the abundant fruit and vegetable operations lining the nearby shores of Lake Erie. He also questioned our real estate agent about New York's tolerance toward home schooling.

"Try it and see," was the agent's response.

My parents proceeded to do so.

School officials first confronted us five months after we arrived in Brocton, New York. At the time, we knew of no other families who attempted to home school in New York, and we had no idea what to expect. However my parents determined to stand on their beliefs, come what may.

Lydia was teaching six of us younger ones at home when school officials came to question Mom. We heard them speak from where we were studying in an upstairs room, and teacher and students fell silent, trying to catch their words. "We have to see to it that these children attend school legally," a woman's voice was stating. Many scenes raced through our minds, including those frequent wearying travels we'd undertaken in our determination to home school. And we pictured a drama of recent years when school officials chased Amish children through an Iowa cornfield, trying to forcibly enroll them in public school.

Challenging the State

Our right to home schooling was challenged even more severely after we moved to a farm in Cassadaga, which was to become our permanent home. The Cassadaga school administrator was greatly annoyed by the presence of this family from out-of-state attempting to defy his previously unchallenged authority. "Child neglect" was the charge he filed against my parents in family court.

The danger of forcible removal from our parents was the only thing we children could not acceptably face. So we banded together and arranged a secret hideout, unknown even to our parents, to which we would flee if the officials ever came for us. We never had to use it.

Acquaintances and employers of ours were vocal in our defense, and the case was thrown out of court, thus demonstrating the power of concerned citizens in reining in oppressive government. Also somewhat influential in our case was a brand-new Supreme Court ruling in favor of Amish families who had objected to public schooling and education beyond the eighth grade for their children.

We cooperated with Cassadaga school officials as far as possible throughout our years of home schooling. Initially we underwent inspections, exams, and interviews. The Cassadaga school principal came to observe our school and concluded of the teacher, "She may not be certified, but she's certainly qualified."

Later on we simply maintained free and friendly communications with school officials. Local teachers offered us their out-of-date books. On several occasions Lydia was even asked by area parents to tutor their children whose public school education was proving insufficient.

After teaching at a mission school in Belize, Central America, for five years, Lydia returned home to teach her own daughter along with several nieces and nephews. Present regulations require her to submit quarterly progress reports on each student to the Cassadaga school. The paperwork aside, she still teaches as she sees best, and with her superior results, no one wants to interfere.

The success of schools such as Lydia's and other private schools is drawing more attention with every new statistic on the disappointing results of public education. I have heard various suggestions advanced by citizens concerned with bringing American education back to par: teach teachers better, return to the three R's, require more hours in school, and so forth. The difference between private and public education, however, involves issues more fundamental than these arguments. It involves the entire student-teacher relationship. Private, competing schools are bound to the individual choices of those whom they serve. Schools bound to mandatory regimens rather than client interests are inherently incapable of providing what I call true education— i.e., knowledge garnered through the inner instincts to inform yourself to your own benefit. There's a difference between this type of knowledge and the kind that is methodically dumped upon you by the state.

Since knowledge that benefits one person may not benefit another, true education is infinitely diverse, varying from methods as ancient and basic as apprenticeship, to the most sophisticated academic instruction.

We as a family are now far from alone as home schoolers in our county and state. Lydia meets and exchanges ideas with a number of other parents who teach their own children. She also subscribes to *The*

Teaching Home magazine, where one can gather or share helpful information as well as insights into national home schooling developments. *The Teaching Home* (P.O. Box 20219, Portland, Oregon 97220–0219) informs us that there are 4,000 children on record as being home schooled in New York State. We know that there are more who are not on the record, perhaps fortunate enough never to be discovered by the educational bureaucracy. All told, there are an estimated 300,000 to 500,000 children being taught at home in the United States (*The New York Times*, November 22, 1990).

The Advantages of Home Schooling

It is from my own experience that I call these children fortunate. If their education bears any resemblance to my own, it will possess several advantages.

First, it will contain a much richer infusion of parental interests, which are more sensitive to a child's individuality and total needs than are bureaucratic state interests.

Another rather marked contrast between public schooling and home schooling involves children's peer relationships. The home-educated child is spending more time with adults and siblings and therefore devotes more mental energy to relationships spanning age and generation gaps. Some parents may not see this as desirable. Others find it offers a healthy alternative to the intense peer pressure in most public schools. Excessive peer pressure can and does inhibit a human being's ability to think freely.

In my own growing-up experience, I spent fewer than average hours with children outside the family, and zero hours watching television. Certainly this restricted my range of interactions with others. It did not, however, restrict my intellectual exercises in the least. I turned to my own unbounded imagination. I turned to exploring everything in sight, including books. Adult books were interesting enough to read cover to cover before I was 10 years old. For some reason, I never experienced, nor could I mentally conceive, the boredom with life displayed by many other youngsters.

Learning is exploration and discovery, whether you are observing the development of an ear of corn, working alongside Mom in the kitchen, going to school at home—or even attending a prestigious university.

A School with a Money-Back Guarantee

by Scott Payne

In Lansing, Michigan, one finds a new wrinkle in education: a money-back guarantee. HOPE Academy, a primary and secondary school operated for profit by Eleanor Sambaer and Marina Farhat makes this unique offer: *Give us your kindergartner. If, by the end of the academic year, your child can't read at least on a second-grade level, you get your money back.*

The guarantee is one means by which HOPE's founders have given a future both to their school and to their dream of offering children an education of the highest caliber. Mrs. Sambaer and Mrs. Farhat began HOPE (Heightened Options in Private Education) because they believe that public schools neither challenge children academically, nor support families' beliefs and moral codes.

That the pair even managed to open HOPE is remarkable. Early on, they discovered that one cannot set up classrooms in, say, an empty store. State and local codes require prohibitively expensive retrofitting of wiring and plumbing, the addition of fire walls and security doors, removal of asbestos, plus a myriad of other requirements having little to do with education.

The women sidestepped these obstacles when they found a home for HOPE in a partly vacated public school dating from the 1930s. Like the school's oak doors and bannisters, the desks exhibit years of battering, but this doesn't concern HOPE's owners. "The amount of money public education wastes on brand-new architecture and pretty new desks is crazy," they say. "Education takes place in the mind. Old desks and 50-year-old buildings don't matter."

When the two women opened HOPE in 1985, half of its first 35 students were black children from inner-city homes—a proportion that persists today. HOPE's enrollment rose to 68 in 1986 and 80 in 1987.

HOPE Academy's teaching methods were inspired by Marva Collins' Westside Preparatory School in Chicago. Mrs. Farhat, in fact, visited Mrs. Collins' school and employs some of the techniques Mrs. Collins has revived from the past:

Mr. Payne is a marketing promotions writer living in Muskegon, Michigan. This article originally appeared in the June 1992 issue of *The Freeman*.

- minute-to-minute teacher contact with each pupil
- strong non-denominational religious emphasis in the curriculum
- reliance upon timeless Western literature from *The Iliad* through *The Little Red Hen*
- use of phonics in reading instruction
- insistence on mastery of standard spoken English, with enforced use of complete sentences in classroom discourse
- relentless emphasis on neatness and proper conduct.

But whereas Marva Collins can subsidize Westside Prep with royalties from her books and fees from her lecture tours, no such resources were available to Mrs. Farhat or Mrs. Sambaer. By the end of 1988, HOPE seemed headed for financial collapse, despite holding costs to $3,000 per student (substantially less than Michigan's public schools). "When I look back on what we went through," Marina Farhat says, "I'm surprised we were able to keep going."

The problem, in part, was that neither woman was trained in business. Mrs. Farhat is a teacher, and Mrs. Sambaer is a nurse. They were offering a unique curriculum, but in the manner of public schools: 8:00 A.M. to 4:00 P.M. daily, nine months a year. Perhaps the only thing keeping HOPE open was its founders' sense of mission.

Farhat and Sambaer wanted HOPE to train the intellect. "We want our children to be able to think and act for themselves in a free society," Marina Farhat says. Whereas public education stresses feelings above reasoning, she says, she and her partner want HOPE to do the opposite. "You can't expect to lead life based on good feelings," Marina Farhat says. "We want children to be able to deal with the things that *don't* make them feel good."

Many parents would agree with that remark, but debates between liberal and conservative educators go over most laymen's heads. Accordingly, a businessman challenged HOPE's owners to stop responding to public education's feel-good jargon. He suggested instead that they focus on all parents' instinctive expectation of education: that their children leave school better equipped for life than were the parents when they completed their own schooling. And the only way parents can assess that, he added, is by observing how their youngsters measure up against other children. The thought chimed with Marina Farhat's feeling that large numbers of parents want their children to attend HOPE to acquire the skills and training the parents themselves did not derive from public education.

Sacrifice and Commitment

Enrolling children at HOPE means sacrifice for most inner-city parents. One working couple with a modest income pays $710 a month in tuition for three daughters—a kindergartner, a first-grader, and a third-grader. The school has no scholarship program, though the HOPE Academy Foundation is a vehicle through which contributors could assist with tuition. Farhat and Sambaer oppose free-ride scholarships, however. They believe direct parental financial commitment contributes to quality schooling.

That impression dovetails with the businessman's perception of preschool and kindergarten as the keys to the school's survival and growth. If parents could discern substantial progress in their children at those school levels, he said, they would not view tuition as a sacrifice—particularly not in the case of HOPE's year-long preschool which isn't available at all through public education. He further challenged Farhat and Sambaer not just to pay lip service to making a profit, but to pursue profit because it is the most reliable feedback. If HOPE is good, he told them, it will earn money. The public schools' product is free, he added, so you've got to show the consumer that their product is not in the same league with yours.

Seeing their school through a businessman's eyes surprised HOPE's owners. They hadn't realized that by adopting public education's 8 to 4 day, they overlooked the convenience of parents, their sole revenue source. They also realized that public education's three-month summer vacation is a remnant of agrarian times that teachers' unions protect as a perk. But for a private school, summer vacation is a heavy cost. Rent and insurance payments don't stop in June—so revenue must not stop, either. Thus, Sambaer and Farhat put HOPE and its teachers on a year-around schedule.

With the help of a consultant, they developed a marketing campaign featuring the money-back guarantee for kindergartners. They also began fitting HOPE's schedule to parents' schedules, 7:00 A.M. to 6:00 P.M., so the school is a home away from home, and HOPE preschoolers and pupils need not be latchkey kids. Enrollment has climbed to 150—still equally divided between suburban and inner-city families—and the school is solvent. In addition to its preschool, HOPE's summer schedule offers remedial training for public school students and accelerated classes for students who want to get ahead.

Summer also is when HOPE screens prospective transfer enrollees to ascertain whether their work habits and academic skills are up to HOPE's level—and, if not, to get them there. "Often we find that public school students just don't have work habits. And their skills aren't at a point that they can handle HOPE's program," Marina Farhat says. "Sometimes we have to tell parents that we must hold their child back a year."

In addition, Sambaer and Farhat are thinking about offering a full summer semester at HOPE. Marina Farhat says parents seem equally divided about enrolling their youngsters in the summer, but she believes that in a year or two HOPE will provide the option.

Meanwhile, she chuckles over the year-long debate in the state capitol about "equalizing" funding for public education's "rich" school districts, which spend $6,000 per pupil per year, and "poor" districts that spend only $4,000.

"With that kind of money. . . ," she grins. "Well, we think we're doing pretty well here with only $3,000."

The Generosity of Americans: A Review

by Richard Christenson

Defenders of the welfare state often base their case on the assumption that few Americans would be inclined to support the necessary educational and welfare needs of our nation, or would lack the means if they had the inclination; government, therefore, has to step in. Mr. Marts, a professional fund raiser, explodes this assumption. He shows that the helping hand has always been extended in America, that the generosity of individuals worked out solutions to all sorts of problems long before government intervened. His historical research traces our tradition of voluntarism, for carrying out good works by personal giving and private philanthropy.

Although many of his examples are lengthy and of only passing interest to the average reader, the author gives an intriguing account of how effective private philanthropy has been and is even now. The American people gave more than $11 billion last year to finance everything from local universities to national arts and science projects; the generosity of Americans is beyond question. Mr. Marts shows that in contrast to Europe and Asia, where philanthropy is practiced by only a few, American generosity is widespread. Last year over 40 million Americans, individuals and families representing all economic levels, made contributions to various causes. This national characteristic is not something new but was in such obvious contrast to Continental practice that Alexis de Tocqueville praised it in his writings over a century ago.

How much would people give if the progressive income tax were abolished? This is an interesting question. An answer is suggested in the data provided by the author concerning the acceleration of private giving in England during the reigns of King Henry VIII and Queen Elizabeth when the Tudor Charitable Laws were first enacted. It was from this beginning that the generous men and women of England started so many projects to help the underprivileged and poor of the nation that it makes our present war on poverty pale by comparison.

Private philanthropy satisfies something deep in the nature of the

---

This review originally appeared in the November 1966 issue of *The Freeman*.[1]

giver, Mr. Marts points out. "For some reasons, unseen and even not fully comprehended (like most spiritual motivations), many generous givers develop giving as a habit; a pleasing and satisfying refinement; a meaningful expression of their personality . . . numerous examples provide eloquent arguments for the critics and seem to show that if anything, giving tends to increase the capacity of individuals to share."

Private philanthropy has also proved to be the most creative and imaginative way of introducing new solutions to social needs: "Private generosity for the public good does [the] pioneering."

The late A. M. Schlesinger, Sr., writes: "In contrast to Europe, America has practically no misers and the consequence of the winning of Independence was the abolition of primogeniture and entail. Harriet Martineau was among those who concluded that 'the eager pursuit of wealth does not necessarily indicate a love of wealth for its own sake.' The fact is, that for a people who recalled how hungry and ill-clad their ancestors had been through the centuries in the Old World, the chance to make money was like the sunlight at the end of a tunnel. It was the means of living a life of human dignity. In other words, for the majority of Americans it was a symbolism of idealism rather than materialism. Hence, this 'new man' had an instinctive sympathy for the underdog, and even persons of moderate wealth gratefully shared it with the less fortunate, helping to endow charities, schools, hospitals, and art galleries and providing the wherewithal to nourish movements for humanitarian reform which might otherwise have died a-borning."

But now government is deep into fields once the domain of private philanthropy. It seems somewhat contradictory that we would go to so much effort to breathe life into something and get it started privately and then allow government with its historic inefficiency to adopt and support the newborn creature. What would happen today if the government's role were reduced, permitting people to keep the dollars now taxed away? In such an unhampered atmosphere of freedom the private sector could once again assume its responsibility for generous giving on even a more massive scale than now.

---

1. Arnaud C. Marts, *The Generosity of Americans* (Englewood Cliffs, NJ: Prentice-Hall, 1966).

The Tragedy of American Compassion: A Review

by Daniel A. Bazikian

Marvin Olasky believes that the present American poverty programs and welfare system have failed, not only in terms of money squandered, but also in regard to human souls corrupted and national character corroded. As a Christian, he argues for a biblical model for fighting poverty. In *The Tragedy of American Compassion* (Washington: Regnery Gateway, 1992), Olasky develops this argument historically, by chronicling and criticizing efforts to fight poverty from colonial times to the present. As he states in his introduction, "The key to the future, as always, is understanding the past."

Olasky argues that indiscriminate government handouts of aid do not better the individual; instead, they merely foster further moral laxity and irresponsibility. Poverty can be alleviated, however, not only as well-to-do individuals help less fortunate individuals, but also as the better-off help the morally and economically downtrodden learn to live out the biblical work ethic in their lives. Personal beliefs and personal values play a determinative role in the economic outcome of one's life.

The early American concept of charity, as expressed from both pulpit and printed page, stressed biblical themes. This established the cultural and intellectual framework for viewing the problem for at least the next 250 years. Charitable aid was encouraged to be given in a spirit of generosity (which in those days was associated with nobility of character, as well as gentleness and humility). Emphasis on a God of justice and mercy, and of man as a fallen, sinful creature, led people "to an understanding of compassion that was hard-headed but warm-hearted." Those in genuine need would be helped, but those who were slothful were allowed to suffer until they showed a willingness to change.

Other strong concepts also emanated from this theistic outlook: Giving was to be done not mechanically but from a spirit of genuine love; almoners of charity were to acquaint themselves personally with the poor, so as to discern better who deserved aid and who did not; moral and spiritual guidance was to be dispensed along with material

Mr. Bazikian is a free-lance writer from Weehawken, New Jersey. This article originally appeared in the December 1993 issue of *The Freeman*.

aid; because men's sinfulness often prompted them to abuse charity, donors were advised to withhold it at times; and giving was done in such a way as to strengthen and encourage family life. Charity of this type not only characterized the predominantly Protestant population, but also the small Catholic and even smaller Jewish minorities as well.

The growth of cities in nineteenth-century American often intensified the needs of the poor. In response, the new world came to look to the old for a workable answer. Scottish theologian Thomas Chalmers, a strong critic of the government-run, indiscriminate "outdoor relief" established in England's newly industrialized cities, adhered basically to the same viewpoint on poverty as his American counterparts. From 1819 to 1823, he devised a plan for implementing his ideas within a specially created, ten thousand-person district (the Parish of St. John) in Glasgow. Within this parish, state, or other indiscriminate aid was excluded and all needed relief was to be met by the donations of parishioners. Chalmers divided his parish into 25 districts, each the responsibility of a deacon who would investigate who were the genuinely needy. The effects reportedly were remarkable: Church charitable giving increased (donors were confident of the wise use of their money); the better-off induced the poor through habits of industry and thrift to improve their lot; and the number of poor in the parish as a consequence shrank.

By around the middle of the century, charitable societies in every major American city were being established mainly along Chalmers' lines. Workers in these organizations shared a view that the underlying causes and long-term needs of the poor were religious. Only when the poor learned to address these needs would they lift themselves (through God's help) out of poverty.

Up to the 1840s, a general consensus still prevailed regarding society's treatment of the poor. Charity was handled mainly through private efforts. Government support of the poor was limited. The English system of indiscriminate state aid to the poor was scorned as degrading to the recipients.

That decade witnessed the first serious challenge to this consensus. Horace Greeley, founder and editor of the *New York Tribune* as well as a theological Universalist and utopian socialist, believed in the natural goodness of man, as well as the corrupting influence of capitalist society. According to Greeley, every person had a right to both eternal salvation and temporal prosperity, and poverty was to be alleviated by redistributing the wealth to everyone without making moral distinctions as to the recipients.

Later in the century came the attack of the Social Darwinists, who viewed the struggle within society in terms of the survival of the economic fittest. Character, they contended, was hereditary, and attempting to lift those poor souls from the grips of vice and poverty was therefore useless. Both of these attacks were ably and articulately confronted by those holding Christian views of charity.

Another and more subtle assault on this consensus was to have a more devastating impact. A new strain of liberalism (referred to as "Social Universalism" by Olasky), combining theological liberalism and political socialism, gained a strong following among the nation's intellectual and literary elite. Theologically, its adherents substituted the notion of God's love for all, for the notion of God's love for his people. Instead of emphasizing charity to individuals, the new emphasis (similar to Greeley's) was on aiding the masses through improvement of their environment. The religiously distinctive principles of traditional charities were also muted or removed. This new charitable outlook found expression in the "settlement house" movement of the 1890s (of which Jane Addams' Hull House in Chicago was the flagship). According to Olasky, this movement would become the inspiration for governmental social work programs of the 1930s and the community action programs of the 1960s. Along with these developments, a new discipline, sociology, was emerging, which would leave its strong imprint on twentieth-century work among the poor. In general, these movements looked to the government as the proper agency to bring about the needed social changes and reforms.

These new currents of thought affected the charitable system in important ways. Professionals, rather than volunteers, would now tend to dominate. The roles of non-professionals would be reduced to that of fund-raising or giving money. This would bring an increasing social separation between donor and recipient. The old compassion (the idea of suffering with the poor) was gone. With the coming of the Great Depression of the 1930s, the private charitable system was overwhelmed, and in stepped the government in the person of FDR and his New Deal.

The advent of the New Deal marked a definitive shift in the federal government's role in respect to society's needy. The cultural ethos of the work ethic, however, remained strong in America. This made it difficult for political leaders to act in terms of direct charitable relief. New Deal programs, therefore, often emphasized their temporary nature, or involved efforts to pay workers for actual work done (e.g., the Works Progress Administration). At the same time, New Deal leaders reiterated their support for the old work ethic. Their pronouncements notwithstanding, a subtle change in public attitudes toward personal responsibility and rugged individualism was taking place.

As late as the 1960s, the cultural bias against welfare still remained, not only among its administrators but also among its recipients. It was left to LBJ's Great Society to breach this cultural wall. Personnel belonging to, or in some way affiliated with, its Office of Economic Opportunity as well as the private National Welfare Rights Organization radicalized the poor so as to demand their full rights or entitlements. The welfare mentality among the poor became firmly implanted, and the number of welfare recipients ballooned.

Olasky's chapter on "The Seven Marks of Compassion" constitutes the heart of his study and of his critique. Seven basic ideas motivated the charity workers of a century ago: *affiliation*, that is keeping the individual's family, religious, or community ties strong so as to strengthen his sense of belonging; *bonding*, or developing a close personal relationship between the charity volunteer and the recipient, in order to coax and encourage the latter to self-sufficient status; *categorization*, or assigning individuals to different categories of need (e.g., the need for continuous relief, relief on a temporary basis, aid in a job search, or just designating someone as unfit for relief due to unwillingness to work); along with this went *discernment*, the willingness to separate worthy objects of charity from fraudulent ones; seeking the goal of long-term *employment* of all able-bodied heads of household so as to instill self-sufficiency and responsibility in the individual; placing emphasis on *freedom*, or the ability to work without governmental restrictions so as to improve one's lot in life over a period of time; finally, recognizing the relationship of the person to *God*, since men and women had spiritual as well as physical needs.

The presence of these principles gave traditional charities their great strength. Conversely, their absence in contemporary charity does so much to explain the spiritual and moral poverty of American compassion and its tragic social consequences: the decline in upward mobility of the poor; the weakened state of private charity; and the disintegrating state of marriage. These principles, Olasky contends, need to be reinserted and reintegrated into programs to aid the poor.

Olasky has set forth his case compellingly and clearly. One hopes that this book will act as a catalyst in bringing about a thorough discussion of the issues involved so that the needs of the poor can be properly addressed.

Charity in the Land of Individualism

by John D. Fargo

It was back on the farm, late 1940s, along the northwestern edge of the corn belt—in the land of individualism. Folks were poor, and only the more rugged had survived the ravages of the Great Depression, but times were better now.

A new farmer moved in and rented the farm across the section. I'll call him George. Within this self-reliant culture, George didn't fit in well. Each farm, a piece of carefully marked-off private property, was conscientiously cared for by the farmer and his family, but not George's.

This was before farmers used chemical weed killers. Thus, each farmer had to control weeds the hard way, by laboriously chopping them down, lest they go to seed and infest not only his field but those of his neighbors. But not George.

We shared three-quarters of a mile of fence with George. Each farmer took care of half his common fences, making repairs when needed and chopping the weeds out of the fence row each summer. But George never laid a hand on any part of that fence.

Thistles were a nasty problem. Patches of these perennial weeds choked out the grain, and with no chemicals they were all but impossible to destroy. In the fall the thistles released thousands of tiny seeds that floated in the wind and could spread for miles. It was understood in the land of individualism that no one let his thistles go to seed—but George exempted himself. His farm became an eyesore in a culture where pride in one's property, rented or otherwise, ran high.

Farmers often had to extend themselves. For example, instead of the normal 12-hour workday, they might put in 15 to 18 hours a day to get the hay crop in before a rainstorm. But George was too irresponsible to put forth the extra effort.

Corn, which requires a relatively long growing season, was the main crop back then, but it was vulnerable along the northwestern edge of the corn belt. Farmers had no commercial grain driers; most of them didn't even have electricity. Thus, to prevent spoilage, the corn

Mr. Fargo is a free-lance writer living in Los Angeles. This article originally appeared in the August 1992 issue of *The Freeman*.

had to be left in the fields until it became sufficiently dry. This meant waiting until October, when early snows threatened to bury the crop.

Every October the race was on—to beat that first snowstorm and get the corn in. Corn-picking machines were repaired, greased, and ready to go. Corn cribs were built, farm kids skipped school to help with the harvest, and the time for 16-hour days, seven days a week, was on. But not George—his dilapidated corn picker wasn't ready. And his three little kids were too young to help bring in the crop.

Tragedy Strikes

Machinery was primitive by today's standards. Corn pickers often broke down, and dry corn husks often wouldn't feed down between the steel husking rollers. Instead, they accumulated above the roller, plugging up the machine. The operator was constantly stopping his machine to dig out the jammed husks. It was a tedious process.

But there was a faster and easier way of handling this problem; leave the machine running, reach in with your hand, and push the husks down so they would feed through the steel-ridged rollers. It was dangerous; a man could lose his fingers.

Well, George did it the easy way. He had barely gotten started with his corn picking when those steel rollers grabbed his finger. All the doctor could salvage of his mutilated right hand was part of one finger and his thumb, minus the nail.

"He probably deserved it." I never heard those words spoken, but I don't doubt that the thought ran through a mind or two. In any event, the forces of selection had weeded George out. Farming required a strong back and two good hands, and this incident ensured that George would never farm again.

Word of the tragedy spread rapidly. The next day, a neighbor drove up to where we were working and talked briefly to my father. The neighbor planned to work in George's fields the following day—maybe get some of his crop in—and thought we might like to help.

Early the next morning, we pulled into George's farm with our corn picker, wagons, elevator (a long conveyor mechanism that lifted the corn into the cribs), and hoist (which lifted the front end of the wagons for easier unloading). George had no permanent corn cribs, so we scrounged around in the dark, looking for pieces of old corn-crib fencing to construct temporary cribs. About then, another farmer pulled in with a trailer loaded with brand new corn-crib fencing.

Before daybreak, we had the elevator up and running, the bottom rung of the corn crib built, and the first loads of corn already were coming in from the fields. The bitter cold penetrated to the bone, and I was anxious to start unloading wagons.

A young farmer drove in with his corn picker, stopped where I was working, and asked if he could help me unload wagons. That seemed strange because running the elevator and hoist, tending the temperamental gasoline engine that powered the works, and unloading the wagons was normally a one-man job. He insisted until I convinced him I could handle it—and they probably needed him and his corn picker in the fields. It wasn't until he left that I realized it was probably my age that had prompted his offer. I was 11 or 12 at the time, but younger kids than I were operating the tractors that pulled the wagons loaded with corn.

Judging by the rate the corn started coming in, I figured there must have been a dozen corn pickers running. A second elevator pulled into the farmyard and was set up nearby. More corn pickers arrived—their faded yellow, green, or red paint showing through the dirt and grime of the machines. By mid-morning the place was swarming with people and machines.

Farm wives drove in with pots and baskets of food for dinner (the noon meal). The area near the farmhouse was beginning to look like a small parking lot. The house could not hold everyone, so we ate in shifts. Most ate quickly and quietly, then returned to work. I didn't know of anyone who was on "visiting terms" with George and his family.

By mid-afternoon, some of the corn pickers were returning from the fields, pulling through the farm yard, and leaving. One farmer, pulling in a load of corn, said that most of the corn was picked and they were starting to get in each other's way. Before dark George's entire crop was harvested, and he hadn't even returned from the hospital.

The remaining operators were solemnly departing. I counted over 20 corn pickers leaving, but there weren't that many farmers in the area. Some of them must have pulled their machines several miles in order to help out. Now, each farmer was going his own way, returning to his own fields where he would work late into the night in that annual race with the snowstorms.

That was how charity worked in the land of individualism, back before the welfare state became entrenched.

It may take the world a while, but eventually it will discover that true charity lies deep within the fertile soil of authentic individualism. These rugged souls, who dare to stand alone, tend to have hearts of gold.

Ending Welfare as They Knew It

by Gerald Wisz

Broadway Presbyterian Church, located in uptown New York City near Columbia University, has always had a place in its heart for the poor people in its community. That's why the church started a soup kitchen in 1980. The indigent, many of whom were drug-addicted and incapable of holding down a job, would come to the church to eat.

As time passed, other organizations—including student groups at Columbia and nearby Union Theological Seminary—also volunteered at the soup kitchen. Before long up to 250 people were eating lunch in the church's basement every day. It had become a sprawling volunteer enterprise. But even its most ardent supporters began to realize something was missing.

Chris Fay, a sexton at the church, and Bill Stewart, one of its members, were among the people at Broadway who felt frustrated with the soup kitchen concept. As the program ballooned, they noticed how the people who frequented the church's facility came only to continue in their self-destructive habits. Lunchers made no visible attempt of using the meals to sustain them until they could afford to feed themselves. For them the soup kitchen had become yet another entitlement; if anything it helped subsidize their dependency.

Aiming for Self-Reliance

In 1990, Stewart came across "The Miserly Welfare State," an article by Marvin Olasky in *Policy Review*. Olasky showed how problem with the welfare state is not that it spends too much on the homeless, but that ultimately it does not—and cannot—spend enough. Minimal stipends and perfunctory bureaucratic counseling are about all the welfare state can provide a growing dependent population. These, Olasky wrote, are poor replacements for personal acts of charity that encourage self-reliance. Charity, as earlier philanthropic organizations understood but contemporary ones have largely forgotten, emphasizes practical measures that help people themselves.

Mr. Wisz is a financial journalist in New York. This article originally appeared in the October 1994 issue of *The Freeman*.

Impressed with the article, Stewart made copies to circulate among the church's board of elders. "The article put into words what many of us were feeling for a long time but couldn't quite articulate or conceive of doing ourselves," said Stewart, who is partner of a shipping-insurance business in midtown. "The responsibility model, instead of the welfare model, is where we knew we had to migrate."

Migrating wasn't easy. The church was divided over the issue, and compromises were made, but in the end most agreed a different approach was needed. The soup kitchen was kept, but with the understanding that it would serve as a gateway to a responsibility-based program for those wanting to change.

Opposition came early from the Presbyterian denomination of which Broadway was a part. The regional and national officers of the Presbyterian Church (U.S.A.) have drifted into a preoccupation with political correctness. Part of Broadway's new plan was Street Smart, a program wherein men visiting the church for food agree to sweep the sidewalks along storefronts on upper Broadway for minimum wage. If they show up for work on time, stay off substances, and cooperate with the program director, they get raises in 25-cent increments. There's also an opportunity for promotion to supervisor. Visiting presbyters from the denomination condemned the program as "racist" since participants are black.

Summoned before the presbytery, program organizer Chris Fay didn't even have to defend himself. John Sligh, one of the Street Smart sweepers, stood before the assembled clergy and elders—many of whom were also black—and told them how the program had taught him the importance of self-sufficiency, which gave him back his self-respect. "He told them we, through the program, probably saved his life," Fay reported. "They didn't have a lot to say after that." Today the New York metropolitan presbytery is among Street Smart's largest financial supporters. In operation for two-and-a-half years, Broadway's program has received only a few thousand dollars of public funds for an art therapy project. The rest is financed by private giving from within and outside the church.

Rewarding Responsibility

The soup kitchen changed. Now fewer people are fed each day, and the church actively encourages visitors to volunteer in preparing, serving, and cleaning up after meals. If they do so, they get food to take home. If their help continues with some consistency, they get a stipend.

Like Street Smart, the kitchen volunteer program also provides avenues for raises and advancement.

There is a Bible study—distinct from Broadway Community, Inc., the nonprofit umbrella organization that runs the program—where participants receive spiritual nurture. The Bible study, like other aspects of Broadway's outreach, is purely voluntary. If there are serious problems like severe drug addiction, however, participants are referred to a city agency.

Broadway has worked with 15 people this year, and of these Moira Ojeda, the program director, said she thinks "seven are going to make it." Two already have jobs outside the church program. Last year, one received his commercial driver's license and is now driving a truck full time.

Participants in the program draw up a "covenant" with Ojeda. They list goals, what they plan to do to accomplish them, and report to Ojeda periodically to review their progress. The covenants are signed, and are expected to be kept. "Once progress is made in achieving a goal, and reported to me and the group at large, we move onto the next one, which is built on the previous one," Ojeda said. What state welfare office, even with all the "two-years-and-out" talk, does this?

Teaching responsibility step-by-step has worked. The numbers are small, but the change in lives seems permanent. But Bill Stewart is not too concerned about the numbers right now.

"While we're sure we won't succeed with everyone, we're sure we'll succeed with many," he said of the two-and-half year-old program. "We're not trying to solve society's problems, but we're trying to develop a model that succeeds with people willing to make a change in their lives—to lift themselves out of alcohol, drugs, degradation, and despair and come back into a community of family, friends, and the working world. If we can point to this and say that it works, we'll spread it as wide and as far as we can."

The Best for Priscilla

by Robert A. Peterson

When our sixth child was born a few months ago, we were distressed to hear that she might have a problem with her hips. Visions of a baby in braces raced through our minds. Trying to be the strong husband, I said to my wife, "Don't worry, we'll get the best for Priscilla."

Our pediatrician advised us to have ultrasound testing to see if Priscilla's legs were joining properly with the hip sockets. He sent us to a hospital especially for children—the Alfred I. duPont Institute in Wilmington, Delaware. I didn't know it at the time, but I was in for a lesson in economics that I'll never forget.

The hospital is on the former estate of American inventor, businessman, and philanthropist Alfred duPont, whose money founded the Institute. A remarkable man from a remarkable family, he inherited a substantial fortune and built it into an even larger sum. Like most duPonts, he worked his way up from the bottom, learning the family business in the powder mills along the Brandywine River. In his later years, he decided to move south and spent his time rebuilding Florida's economy after the boom and bust real estate deals of the 1920s. His holdings eventually included forests, banks, railroads, and real estate. His rule: invest only for long-term growth. In fact, duPont didn't expect to reap rewards from his investments during his lifetime.

When he died in 1935, he left an estate of some $70 million. Nearly half—$30 million—was consumed in state and Federal inheritance taxes. After leaving a few million to his wife and children, the remainder endowed the Nemours Foundation, which was charged with opening a hospital devoted to children. For nearly 60 years, the foundation has been benefiting children, operating with funds earned from profitable investments in America's free enterprise system. The hospital, which has never turned a child away, represents the best in free enterprise and philanthropy.

DuPont's grounds and mansion are beautiful, but it was the hospital that astonished me. It is a cross between Disney World and a high-tech research center. The receptionist told us that it was especially

Mr. Peterson is headmaster of The Pilgrim Academy in Egg Harbor City, New Jersey. This article originally appeared in the May 1992 issue of *The Freeman*.

designed to be non-threatening to children. The interior of each wing is decorated in a different color—bright red, green, yellow, or blue.

We carried little Priscilla past playroom after playroom and finally reached the ultrasound room. With its soft lighting and colorful aquarium, the room was far from institutional. On the wall were posters of Pinocchio, Snow White, Bambi—cartoon creations from the studio of American artist-entrepreneur Walt Disney. Suspended from the ceiling were more cartoon characters, originally marketed to make a profit for their creators, but who have since delighted—and sometimes comforted—a generation of Americans. Here, also, were doctors and nurses who really cared. Little Priscilla was too young to be impressed by all this, but it sure eased my mind!

The ultrasound imaging took only a few minutes. As we waited for the results and the specialist's opinion, I picked up some literature and began reading more about this wonderful hospital.

At duPont a pre-operative visit helps young surgical patients feel at home and overcome their fears about the procedures they will undergo. They meet "Mr. Teddy Bear," another patient (whose intravenous tube is connected to a bottle of "Hospital 7-Up"), receive a "real" surgical mask, and may take a ride in the red wagon that will transport them to the operating room. As a result, patients are happier, calmer, and easier to help—and so are the parents, who take these things harder than the children do.

On surgery day, the family remains together in a cheerfully decorated room. The patient may play, read, or watch TV until—with a favorite toy or blanket in hand—he is taken to surgery. After surgery, the child is immediately reunited with his parents. More important, the adults are often relieved to find that every anesthesiologist is also certified in pediatrics.

Searching for Tomorrow's Cures

The Nemours Foundation is funding a number of research projects that will benefit the next generation of children. The Institute already is a leader in Lyme disease detection and treatment. Institute scientists also are searching for the causes of muscular dystrophy. So far, researchers have discovered that the chemical compound hemin, when injected into laboratory animals, dramatically increases muscle strength and significantly reduces the invasion of connective tissue cells seen in the disease. Human tests will follow.

The Institute also is adapting computer technology to assist disabled children. Portable robotic arms are being developed that can be placed at a work station or on the side of a wheelchair. These arms then will be programmed to perform specific functions.

Computer devices also are being developed to aid children with speech and hearing impairments. Projects include a telephone system for the deaf that uses video sign language and a speech synthesizer that reflects the age and personality of the user.

The Institute's ultimate goal is to "prolong and improve the lives of children everywhere." But the Institute can't do that without the benefits of a free society. A free society generates the wealth needed to fund continued treatment and research, and provides the climate needed for innovation, discovery, and experimentation.

Today, Alfred duPont's Nemours Foundation continues to invest in profit-seeking enterprises, with the proceeds supporting the hospital's programs. Interest, profits, capital accumulation—things so disparaged by Marx and his followers—are what make the duPont Institute possible. Destroy the profit motive and you throw the baby out with the bath water. Destroy the businesses in which the Nemours Foundation invests and you destroy the Institute. The more business is regulated, the fewer dividends are available to maintain and expand the hospital.

After about a half hour, two doctors came in and gave us their analysis of the ultrasound: Priscilla was okay. There would be no need for a cast, a brace, or any treatment whatsoever. Her hip sockets were fine.

As we were leaving, I asked a hospital administrator if there were any hospitals like this outside the Western world.

"None," she said.

"Have you ever had visitors from Eastern Europe or the Soviet Union?" I asked.

"Yes, as a matter of fact we had some visitors from Russia just a few weeks ago. When they saw what we had here, they wept."

These visitors knew that they could never have such a hospital until their country is free. No amount of central planning, Western subsidies, socialized medicine, or national health insurance could create a duPont Institute. Only the continuing vitality of a free society, where people can innovate, create, invest, and serve others as they choose, makes such an institution possible.

There are many arguments for the free society, but none so compelling as the health and welfare of our children. The best for our little Priscilla—the best for children everywhere—is the fruit of freedom.

Friendly Societies: Voluntary Social Security—And More

by John Chodes

In his retirement speech as Speaker of the House, Tip O'Neill contrasted the world of small government in the 1930s, when he entered politics, with today's big government emphasis on social services, which he helped create: "Health insurance was out of the question. For the elderly, life was filled with uncertainty, dependency and horror. Only the lucky few had pensions. There was no such thing as social security."[1]

O'Neill was wrong. Working class families had a "safety net" long before Uncle Sam became involved. Our grandparents and even great-grandparents had benefit plans that protected them when they were sick, injured, out of work, or too old to work. Millions of workers belonged to "friendly societies."

Various forms of friendly societies have existed since ancient China, Greece, and Rome. In Britain, they arose out of the guild system. Daniel Defoe wrote in 1697 that friendly societies were "very extensive" in England. In the mid-18th century, as the Industrial Revolution hastened the growth of British towns, the friendly society system became well established. Sometimes they were called fraternal societies, mutual aid societies, or benefit clubs. Similar organizations developed in the United States in the 19th century.

The lengthy success of the friendlies reflects that they were much more than benefit institutions. Friendlies were voluntary self-help associations, organized by the members themselves. The workers regarded the friendlies with great pride, as their own creation. More than just a means of support, they brought independence from the degradation of charity.

Friendlies served social, educational, and economic functions, bringing the idea of insurance and savings to those who might not have planned for the future. The social aspect of the friendlies should not be underestimated. Their meetings included lectures, dramatic performances, and dances both to inform and to entertain members.

Mr. Chodes is the Communication Director for the Libertarian Party of New York City. This article originally appeared in the March 1990 issue of *The Freeman*.

Since members took turns at managing the friendlies, the typical workingman developed executive skills that could prove valuable in his everyday employment.

Nineteenth-century commercial insurance companies couldn't compete with the friendlies, so they focused on business clients and the rich. Workers were suspicious of the companies because of their numerous failures and scandals. Besides, insurance rates were higher than those the friendlies charged for comparable benefits. The reason? Friendlies didn't solicit. Thus, there were no salesmen and no commissions. Also, the member-managers worked on a volunteer or token salary basis.[2]

Types of Friendlies

Friendlies usually were formed by people with a common denominator, like the same occupation or same ethnic, geographic, or religious background. Thus, there were the Czechoslovak Society of America, Providence Association of the Ukranian Catholics in America, Locomotive Engineers Mutual Life and Accident Insurance Association, and the Fraternal Society of the Deaf.[3]

Unlike today's compulsory and standardized state-run plans, friendlies provided dozens of benefit packages. Each person created his own plan. One could retire at 60 or even 50 or get unemployment or illness aid equal to one's own wages. All that was required was higher premiums.[4]

Originally, friendlies insured against "disability to work," with little distinction between accident or sickness. This also came to mean "infirmity," i.e., insurance against old age. Most friendlies paid for a doctor's services, burial expenses, annuities to widows, and educational expenses for orphans. They built old-age homes and sanitariums for members and their families. Even in their early stages, they offered unemployment benefits for those in "distressed circumstances" or "on travel in search of employment." The most common pay-outs were for maternity leave and retirement pensions.[5]

1. Dividing Societies

These were among the earliest British friendlies, developing in the 1750s. After making payments for specified "events" (sickness, retirement, death, unemployment), the society would divide the balance of its fund among it members at the end of the year. The disadvantage of this was the constant need to recruit young people because these societies had no reserves, and the bulk of their claims tended to come from older members.

Still their appeal was considerable. Each contributor received an annual return even when things were going well. The fees were uniform and easy to calculate. They used no actuarial tables (which were considered morbid for predicting the odds of sickness and death). The contributions were higher than at other types of friendlies, but the members got back a lump sum at the end of the year. Dividing societies combined insurance with the idea of savings. As such, they advanced loans to members.

A good example of a dividing friendly was the Union Provident Sick Society. In 1880 its rules provided that no one would be admitted under age 16 or over 31. A 12-man executive committee was rotated among the society's members. Meetings were held "every quarter night." There were a small entrance fee and a small contribution every two weeks. Eighty percent went into the fund, 20 percent toward management. Sick benefits were roughly 25 to 33 percent of weekly wages for a year, and 15 to 20 percent for the remainder of the illness. For members over the age of 20, contributions and benefits were double. The surplus was divided each December, the members receiving shares in proportion to their contributions.

Five percent of the Union Provident's members were self-employed tradesmen or manufacturers who didn't need the society's help. They had been workingmen when first admitted, but still remained to show their moral commitment and to donate their managerial skills to the society.

Friendlies that did not divide gave higher benefits. One example was the Hitchen Friendly Institution. It provided benefits equal to full pay for a year to a member who was out of work due to illness, and half pay for the remainder of the illness.[6]

2. Deposit Societies

An English clergyman, Reverend Samuel Best, originated this more sophisticated system. He introduced the concept of savings to early industrial workers. The deposit system connected the savings account with an insurance account so that the benefits for sickness or distress were derived partly from each. The member had a specific credit in the insurance fund based on his savings, but the claim ceased as soon as his own fund was exhausted. This promoted thrift by encouraging the member to add to his savings, not to drain off the account.

If a person remained healthy throughout his working life, when he retired he would have a large amount in his personal account. With much sickness and exhausted savings, the sickness or distress benefits ended, but were replaced by "grace pay," which could be drawn for as long as benefits had been drawn. Grace pay related to the amount of savings.

The deposit system had major advantages over others. It did not use actuarial tables, which would force higher contributions on the elderly or sick, or exclude them from membership. Admission was without limitation.[7]

3. Burial Societies

This was the one area where commercial insurance companies competed successfully because the "event" (death) was easy to verify and actuarially predictable. For a long time burial societies were illegal because they "gambled on death."[8]

4. Factory Societies

There is a widespread belief that the nineteenth-century factory owner was heartless, providing no benefits for his workers. That picture is false, as evidenced by this report from an 1891 study of workingmen's associations: "There is scarcely a single large establishment . . . which does not make provision for its employees, whether accident, sickness or burial. The management is in the hands of the workingmen, while the firm acts as treasurer, exercising some supervision, and represents a moral influence through its chief officers. Membership was supported by the firm. These subsidies gave substantial benefits for small contributors."[9] Another study noted that "the mill owners have created a fund, applied to the encouraging of women to cease work for a sufficiently long time before and after the birth of their children to prevent injury to the constitutions of mother or infant."[10]

5. Building Societies

Building societies were workingmen's financial institutions. They lent money to members for the purpose of buying a home. The "terminating" type ceased existence when all the members had bought a residence. The "permanent" type had more of the characteristics of a contemporary bank.

These societies had a powerful influence until fairly recently. Between 1918 and 1939, half of the homes built in England were purchased with the aid of building society funds.[11]

6. Fraternal Societies

"Fraternals" were more like life insurance companies in that they tended to focus on death benefits and pensions. Because of this, in the long run they were more easily absorbed by the large commercial insurance organizations.

There were dozens of variations of fraternals. Those with branches (or lodges) were commonly called "affiliated" or "federated" orders, with divisions of power between the central administration and the regional branches. Those without branches were referred to as "unitary" societies.[12]

Downfall of the Friendlies

The friendlies did not collapse financially. Nor did they disappear because they failed to do their job for working people. They declined because of government action.

British aristocrats feared the friendlies because they viewed their huge contributor funds as a means for political subversion. At the end of the 18th century, the aristocrats, dreading the political power of the united workers, moved against them. The Combination Acts, the Illegal Societies Act, and the Seditious Meetings Act were aimed at preventing workingmen's groups from forming. The one legal loophole was the Rose Act of 1793, which allowed "societies of good fellowship for security" to exist.[13]

Eventually, a steadily growing web of uniform state-mandated benefits first duplicated, then absorbed the "dangerous" friendlies.

1793: State supervision of friendly societies' management and rules.

1818: First bill to set up a standard of "scientific" contribution rates. This made the fees more uniform, weakened competition, and led to the gradual absorption of the smaller friendlies by the larger.

1870-75: A royal commission studied the friendlies. Parliament created a rival state-run system, focusing on the most predictable "events": burial and retirement benefits.

1911: National Insurance Act. State benefits were expanded, financed by compulsory contributions from employer and employee. Via subsidies, the friendlies were led to administer the state plan. Claims for benefits had to be filed with both systems.

1946-48: The Labour government ended the National Insurance Act subsidies and bypassed the friendlies, structuring a complete and exclusive administrative machine of its own. The loss of funding and higher state benefit rates drove many friendlies out of existence.[14]

In the United States, the government was less worried about the friendlies. The first major legislation, in 1893, was promoted by the friendlies themselves. They lobbied in Washington through the National Fraternal Congress. This organization represented 100 friendly societies with 6 million members and $7 billion in insurance funds. It pressed for passage of the "Uniform Bill," forcing all new friendlies to adopt the same mortality rates. This would put them at a competitive disadvantage to the established societies. However, instead of driving off the upstarts, this legislation blurred the distinction between friendlies and commercial life insurance companies. Legally they were grouped together. As a result, the commercial insurance companies gradually absorbed the friendlies, leaving consumers with fewer choices.[15]

---

1. Thomas P. O'Neill Jr., "When Government Was a Friend in Need" (*The New York Times*, May 16, 1986), p. A-35.

2. Walter Basye, *History and Operation of Fraternal Insurance* (Rochester: The Fraternal Monitor, 1919), pp. 41-52.

3. Richard DeRaismes Kip, *Fraternal Insurance in the United States* (Philadelphia: College Offset Press, 1953), p. 10.

4. Richard Price, *Observations on Reversionary Payments* (London: T. Caldwell and W. Davis, 1803), pp. 141–42.

5. J. M. Baerneither, *English Associations of Workingmen* (London: Swansonnerchem and Co., 1891), p. 164.

6. *Ibid.*, pp. 171-78.

7. William Henry Beveridge, *Voluntary Action* (New York: Macmillan and Co., 1948), pp. 45-50.

8. *Ibid.*, pp. 53-58.

9. Baerneither, pp. 201-05.

10. Michael Cross, editor, *The Workingman in the 19th Century* (Toronto: Oxford University Press, 1974), p. 75.

11. Beveridge, pp. 96-101.

12. Basye, pp. 122-32 and Beveridge, pp. 34-36.

13. Beveridge, p. 63.

14. *Ibid.*, pp. 63-84.

15. Basye, pp. 113-22.

Lodge Doctors And The Poor

by David T. Beito

Medical Care Before the Welfare State, 1900–1930

On the face of it, a historical study of fraternal societies seems to be a subject fit only for connoisseurs of the arcane. Few Americans these days come into contact with such groups. When many of us hear the word *lodge,* we think of it as a place where television characters from our youth, such as Ralph Kramden (of the Loyal Order of Raccoons) and Fred Flintstone (of the Loyal Order of Water Buffalos), escaped from their more sensible wives to engage in childish hijinks—parading around with silly hats and mouthing pretentious rituals.

There was a time, however, when fraternal societies could not be so easily dismissed. Before the rise of the welfare state, they were rivaled only by churches as organizational providers of social welfare. By conservative estimates eighteen million American men and women were members in 1920—at least three out of every ten adult males. While fraternal societies differed in ethnicity, class, and gender, most shared a common set of characteristics. In general, this included a decentralized lodge system, some sort of ritual, and the payment of cash benefits in times of sickness and death.

By the turn of the century, an increasing number of societies began to add treatment by a doctor to their menu of services. This arrangement was known as lodge practice. It involved a simple contract under which a physician provided care in exchange for an annual salary determined by the size of lodge membership. To qualify, a prospective lodge doctor had to win an election by the members. Generally lodge practice plans did not extend beyond basic primary care and minor surgery, although a few provided hospitalization.

Lodge practice became particularly extensive in urban and industrial centers. In 1915, for example, Dr. S. S. Goldwater, Health Commissioner of New York City, went so far as to assert that in many communities it had become "the chosen or established method of dealing with sickness among the relatively poor." In the Lower East Side of

Dr. Beito is Assistant Professor of History at the University of Alabama. This article originally appeared in the May 1994 issue of *The Freeman.*

New York City, he noted, 500 physicians catered to Jewish societies alone. Among blacks in New Orleans there were over 600 fraternal societies with lodge practice during the 1920s.

Nationally, the two leading providers of lodge practice among native whites were the Foresters and the Fraternal Order of Eagles. By 1910, both organizations had over 2,000 doctors under contract to look after the medical needs of about 600,000 members. Yet, aside from the common thread of lodge practice, the Foresters and Eagles were actually quite unalike as fraternal societies.

The Foresters

The Foresters traced their origins directly to the Ancient Order of Foresters, a British organization. The ritual drew inspiration from Robin Hood and his legendary adventures in Sherwood Forest. In keeping with the medieval motif, the lodges were called "courts" and the supreme leader a "chief ranger." Both women and men could join (although in separate courts) and the only tests for membership were belief in a supreme being and good moral character.

Foresters were quintessential internationalists. In an age of self-conscious Anglo-Saxon exclusivity, they were notable among fraternal societies for seeking converts not only in Europe but also in Asia. The chief ranger for over two decades was a Dr. Oronhyatekha, a Canadian Mohawk. Equally remarkable for the time, his ancestry was not a cause of embarrassment for the members; in fact, they wore it as a badge of distinction. One member boasted that "There is not a Forester in the wide world but knows that this full-blooded Indian chief is the one man to whom the Order should be thankful for its wonderful growth."

The Eagles

While the Foresters eschewed nationalism, their leading rival for lodge practice, the Fraternal Order of Eagles, was almost a caricature of apple-pie Americanism. The Eagles opened their first lodge in Seattle, Washington, in 1898. The members embraced a fun-loving and informal style quite unlike more solemn co-fraternalists, such as the Free Masons. The aeries (as Eagles called their lodges), with their well-stocked bars, often served double duty as local community centers. This freewheeling behavior earned the Eagles an unsavory reputation in some quarters. In 1910, *McClure's Magazine* characterized the group as "a great national organization of sporting men, bartenders, politicians, thieves, and professional criminals." The Eagles later refurbished this unwholesome image somewhat by launching a highly visible, and ultimately successful, campaign for the proclamation of Mother's Day.

Less than ten years after the Eagles had been founded, they became noted (notorious in medical society circles) for engaging in lodge practice. For one dollar a year, a member and immediate family could receive basic medical services (including minor surgery). This fee did not pay for treatment for obstetrics, venereal disease, and "any sickness or injury caused or brought about by the use of intoxicating liquors, opiates or by any immoral conduct."

Ladies Friends of Faith

Unfortunately, primary data from individual societies with lodge practice is in very short supply. Nevertheless, some records survive which can shed light on the subject. Particularly helpful is a minute-book from the Ladies Friends of Faith Benevolent Association, covering the period from August 1914 through September 1916. It was a black female society of about 170 members which operated in New Orleans during the early twentieth century.

The Ladies Friends of Faith was not exceptional, at least within the broad context of New Orleans. It was only one of numerous such societies which offered lodge practice to blacks in the city. Among these were local affiliates of two prominent national organizations, the Eastern Star and the Household of Ruth. Much more common, however, were home-grown societies such as the Female Union Band, Young Men of Inseparable Friends, Francs Amis, Holy Ghost, and the United Sons and Daughters. A simple reading of 134 organizational names from a list assembled in 1937 indicates that no less than 40 catered primarily to females.

In terms of organizational structure and benefits, the Ladies Friends of Faith also fit the general local pattern. The rank-and-file voted in annual elections to choose a "society " druggist, doctor, and undertaker who provided services at a low flat rate. Those taken sick collected two dollars a week if they saw the lodge doctor and three dollars if they did not. To guard against false claims for cash benefits and to provide companionship, a visiting committee sat at bedside with the recipient. Those members derelict in these duties had to pay a one-dollar fine.

In this two-year period, the minute-book evidences great activity. One hundred and thirteen individuals (slightly over half the membership) collected sick benefits. Of these, 70 used the lodge doctor at least once; several a dozen times or more. Almost all these applicants obtained cash payments and medical service (including free medicine) without eliciting complaints from the other members.

This does not mean that the deliberation process of the Ladies Friends of Faith was without controversy. Most notably there was a persistent need to grapple with appeals from individuals who had fallen in arrears. At nearly every meeting, the society heard at least one plea from a member unable to pay because of unemployment or poor health. One of the most desperate of these concerned a woman who was "out of Doors, and had no money." In such cases, the society was generally ready to extend help. It allowed 24 members extra time to pay off their debts while it passed the hat for ten others. Not once did the Ladies Friends of Faith reject any of these appeals outright. Such liberality did not translate into open season on the lodge's treasury, however. Those delinquents who failed to explain their "unfinancial" status were readily dropped from the rolls.

Regardless of religious, ethnic or political orientation, all fraternal societies, to the extent they relied on lodge practice, faced a similar set of obstacles. Without a doubt, the most serious was the organized opposition of doctors. By the first decade of the twentieth century, the spread of what became known to critics as the *lodge practice evil* elicited almost universal condemnation among medical societies.

At its core, this opposition represented fear for the future survival of the dominant fee-for-service remuneration. Writing in the *Wisconsin Journal of Medicine*, Dr. W. F. Zierath of Sheboygan, Wisconsin, put the matter succinctly when he chided certain fellow members of the profession for bowing so readily to "the keen business instinct of the laity" who have "discovered in contract practice a scheme to obtain medical services for practically nothing . . . they are organizing societies by the score with that feature as the excuse for their existence." Once doctors allowed themselves to be placed on a fixed payment system, he warned, loss of both income and independence would soon follow. The profession would then become tainted and demoralized by every doctor's cutthroat and undignified scramble to sell to the lowest bidder. Another opponent predicted that lodge practice, if not stopped, would depress fees to levels "comparable to those of the bootblack and peanut vendor."

Lodge elections were depicted as carnivals of corruption in which victory went to those doctors best able to ingratiate themselves with key players in the leadership through extravagant promises or outright bribery. Even when outright corruption did not occur, the critics portrayed the election campaign as dominated by unseemly wire-pulling and backslapping. According to Dr. Zierath, success of a candidate depended upon "the handshaking, the button-holing, the treating to cigars and drinks in public houses."

According to these critics, however, lodge practice was not only bad for doctors, but it also harmed the patient. While they conceded that the fees were low, they warned that the service given in return was shabby. Along these lines, a leading professional journal condemned lodge practice as a vain attempt by the patient to get "something for nothing."

Who Benefited?

Lodge practice, in my view, merits a far more favorable assessment than it received either from contemporary critics or more recent historians. At first blush, such a contention would seem impossible to defend. Most of the surviving sources on which the historian must rely already have turned in a ringing verdict of guilty. This research problem is not fatal, however. Ironically, the strident manifestos published in the medical journals contain a wealth of information which can cast a positive light on lodge practice. With great profit, these professional critiques can be supplemented and compared to the still extant defenses written by doctors and leaders of fraternal societies.

The most important beneficiary of lodge practice was, of course, the patient of modest means. He or she was able to obtain the care of a doctor for about two dollars a year—roughly equivalent to a day's wage for a laborer. If translated into 1994 dollars, this annual fee would be equivalent to about 14 dollars, the hourly wage of some construction workers today!

The remuneration paid to the lodge doctor was a far cry from the higher fee schedules favored by the profession. A local medical society in Pennsylvania was typical in setting for its members the following *minimum* fees: one dollar per physical examination, surgical dressing, and housecall (daytime) and two dollars (nighttime). Such prices, at least for continual service, would have been out of reach for many poor Americans.

Why were the lodges able to charge such low fees? The answer to this question lies with several organizational strengths peculiar to the fraternal structure itself. The fact that lodges could entice doctors with a large and stable market left them well positioned, as one opponent put it, to purchase medical services at wholesale and sell at retail.

Also exerting downward pressure on fees were lodge elections.

While the election process was not without flaws, there is also ample evidence from both supporters and opponents that, on balance, it served members well. It gave patients an opportunity once a year to compare notes on the medical records of both the challenger and incumbent. John C. McManemin, the Past Worthy President of the Eagles, maintained that as "the members have the right of franchise in electing the lodge physician, so have they in deposing him, and it therefore results that unless the physician so selected, attends to the duties devolving upon him he is quickly brought to account." From a very different perspective, a leading opponent of lodge practice complained that during campaigns "colleagues and rival applicants are roundly 'knocked' and their mistakes and capabilities held up to public ridicule and censure."

Quality of Service

Closer inspection of the medical journals also gives some cause to be skeptical of blanket claims that lodges heedlessly sacrificed quality to elect the candidate bidding the lowest fee. The contrary, in fact, occurred in a campaign described by lodge practice adversary Dr. George S. Mathews of Rhode Island:

> ... in one lodge two members in good standing in the State Medical Society openly in lodge meeting underbid [each other]. One volunteered his services at $2 a head. The other dropped his price to $1.75. The first bidder then acceded to this price with medicines furnished. This occasioned a drop in bidder No. 2 in his price to include medicine and minor surgery. To the vast credit of the lodge neither bid was accepted but a non-bidder was given the job at $2.

Even the detractors, while generally disdainful of the quality of care provided, acknowledged that fraternal societies attracted some doctors of ability and high training. In Dr. Goldwater's opinion, for example, there were "many competent medical men and between the slip-shod service of the poor kind of dispensary, and the painstaking care of the conscientious lodge doctor, the choice easily lies with the latter." It is worthy of note that the hack often inspired less contempt than the physician with a lucrative private practice who took a lodge contract on the side. One leading critic excoriated such individuals as "inordinately selfish and avaricious men who have no neighbors in the profession, for they are not Samaritans by practice."

Proprietary Medical Schools

Also misleading were efforts to dismiss the abilities of lodge doctors by citing their low level of medical education. For many opposed to the system, it was merely sufficient to note that these doctors graduated disproportionately from the ranks of the proprietary medical schools. While as a description of reality this was probably accurate, it fails as an indictment. To understand why, a bit of background about proprietary education might be helpful.

These schools had two salient features. First, they were owned by doctors in regular practice and second, unlike the endowed university, they subsisted entirely on tuition. The owners earned income both from tuition received in exchange for delivering lectures and from sometimes lucrative referrals tendered by grateful graduates. The students often came from modest backgrounds and thus lacked both the contacts and financial pull enjoyed by many of their counterparts in the universities. The alumni of these proprietary schools would have ample incentives to be attracted to lodge practice. For a recent graduate especially, a contract with a fraternal society might be the only means available to obtain the necessary financing and community contacts needed to build up a practice.

To call these doctors *quacks*, however, as many critics did, would be a misnomer, at least in the strict meaning of the term. Like every other aspiring doctor, they needed to receive state certification to practice. By no means was this pro forma. Since the 1880s and 1890s, the requirements had become increasingly stringent and failure rates were high. In short, the lodge doctor may not always have been top-of-the-line but he or she had at least rudimentary training.

As the purchaser of these services, the fraternal society also had incentives to maintain the quality of care. An incompetent or arbitrary doctor could prove fatal to actuarial soundness. Moreover, if fraternal advertisements are any indication, prospective members were leery of organizations with high mortality rates. The publicity for the Foresters repeatedly contrasted the death rate of its members (6 per 1,000) with that of the same age group in the general population (9 per 1,000). It credited this low mortality to "Sherlock-Holmes-like acuteness in the detection of bad risks" exhibited by the doctors attached to its courts. This boast was more than hyperbole. In the first decade of the twentieth century, the doctors of the Foresters annually rejected between ten and twenty percent of all initiates.

Additionally to ensure quality of care lodges often imposed specific sanctions, in the form of fines, for doctors who neglected their duties. Among the possible infractions were failure to report at meetings, fraudulent approval of sick claims, and refusal to respond to a patient's housecall. For the latter violation, for example, both the Eagles and Foresters authorized a lodge to hire a substitute from the open market and then deduct the charges from the salary of the delinquent lodge doctor.

An important consequence of lodge practice for the patient was to facilitate habits of assertiveness. The members who used these services anticipated by several decades the *active patient* now very much in vogue. Many physicians, obviously unaccustomed to such treatment, denounced the willingness of members to quibble about fees and diagnosis. One doctor blamed excessive and unnecessary housecalls for engendering fears in the doctor "that he will lose his position if he fails to answer every call regardless of circumstances and his knowledge of the fact that he is being imposed on constantly by members who abuse their privileges."

For the patient, if not always the doctor, lodge practice had the additional virtue of affording accessible preventive care. Again, one need look no further for evidence than the repeated accusations in the professional journals that doctors were being pestered with trivial ailments. According to Dr. Zierath, the patient called on the lodge doctor at all hours of the night "to see cases repeatedly where a physician would not be called, were the regular fee to apply. One of the children in a family has abdominal pain, and the anxious mother promptly conjectures that it is appendicitis" when it was nothing more "than too much indulgence in mince pie. But it looks stylish to have the doctor's rig standing in front of house and excites the curiosity and envy of the neighbors, therefore the 'free' doctor is summoned."

For fraternal societies, by contrast, the ability to readily call on the doctor for any complaint was a major selling point. Lodge practice, wrote a leader of the Eagles, "accords perfectly with the modern theory of the prevention of disease. . . . Many of the poorer members, under other circumstances might delay in calling a doctor until the disease made considerable headway."

Lodge practice opened up rare opportunities for many working-class Americans to compare and experiment and empowered them with the necessary economic clout to break free from the confining view that health care was merely a generic good. It gave patients the wherewithal to use medical services more as a varied menu of choices, each adjustable to suit the particular need at hand.

The discernment of lodge patients was exemplified by their selective patronization of medical services. They may have readily turned to their lodge doctor for prevention, for example, but many looked elsewhere for a cure. On this note, an exhaustive study of blacks in New Orleans, who were members of fraternal societies during the 1930s, found that while 56 percent relied exclusively on the doctor hired by their lodge, the rest also hired private physicians in some cases. A member of one of these societies expressed a typical view when he commented, "Well, I think there is nothing better than a society for when you're sick they give you the best possible attention, but if I were real sick I'd prefer calling a doctor not connected with a society, so that I could get the best of attention. Society doctors are too busy to handle extreme illnesses."

Decline of Lodge Practice

Even before the Depression, lodge practice had begun to fall into a state of decline. The pressure exerted by the leaders of organized medicine hastened the demise. By the 1910s, doctors had launched an all-out war against lodge practice. Throughout the country, medical associations imposed a range of sanctions against lodge doctors, including expulsion from the association and denial of hospital facilities. In certain instances, campaigns were organized to deny patient care, even in emergencies, to members of offending lodges. Most commentary from both sides of this conflict indicates that these sanctions were highly effective. In any case, by the end of the 1930s, the once vibrant health care alternative of lodge practice, which less than two decades before had inspired trepidation throughout the medical establishment, had virtually disappeared.

IV. BASES OF A DYNAMIC ECONOMY

The Forgotten Private Bankers

by Richard Sylla

What is a private banker? Or rather, since the species has more or less disappeared, what was a private banker? Private bankers, to American banking historians, were individuals and organizations that engaged in the business of banking without first obtaining a permit to do so from governmental authorities. As a consequence, the private banker often was free to practice the banking trade with little or no governmental regulation. That was one of the private banker's principal advantages. But it also became a leading reason for the private banker's undoing and eventual disappearance from the economic scene.

Today, when nearly every U.S. (and foreign) bank operates under a license from, and is regulated by, one or more governments, the idea that the provision of banking services could be left to market forces might strike many people as somewhat bizarre and perhaps even dangerous. Nonetheless, this idea was central to the development of the banks and banking systems of England and continental Europe during much of the seventeenth, eighteenth, and nineteenth centuries. The celebrated Rothschilds, for example, were private bankers, and so were all the banks of England—except the Bank of England—until the second quarter of the nineteenth century.

Prominent U.S. Private Bankers

Given the new world's roots in the old, it is not surprising that the idea and the practice of unlicensed, unregulated banking would migrate to the United States. Indeed, a number of the leading figures and financial institutions in U.S. history were private bankers and banks. Alexander Hamilton was instrumental in founding the Bank of New York as a private bank in 1784, although less than a decade later the bank applied for and received a charter from the state of New York. This venerable American institution still carries on its business from its

Dr. Sylla is Henry Kaufman Professor of the History of Financial Institutions and Markets and Professor of Economics at the Stern School of Business, New York University, and a Research Associate of the National Bureau of Economic Research. This article originally appeared in the April 1995 issue of *The Freeman*.

headquarters at 48 Wall Street. Across the street, at 59 Wall Street, is Brown Brothers Harriman & Co., the only remaining private bank of any size in the United States; it is the exception that probes the rule that banks ought to be licensed corporations. This bank began its career in Philadelphia in 1818 as the Merchant Bank of Brown Brothers, with representative branches in Baltimore and London. It moved its headquarters to New York in 1825.

At 60 Wall Street, next to the Bank of New York, are the headquarters of J.P. Morgan & Company. The Morgan bank is now a corporation, but it was a private bank during the time of its legendary founder, John Pierpont Morgan (1837–1913), and it remained so long after his passing. Another noted private bank was the Bank of Stephen Girard in Philadelphia. Girard, possibly the wealthiest American of his era, operated this bank from 1812 until his death in 1831. Girard's bank took over the building of the first federal Bank of the United States after that institution passed out of existence in 1812. The structure still stands as a prominent feature of Independence National Historical Park in Philadelphia.

Extent of Private Banking

Most of America's private bankers were not as large or as prominent as the ones identified here. But they were quite numerous in U.S. history, especially in the early decades. In 1856, U.S. Treasury Secretary James Guthrie reported to Congress on a survey of the extent of private banking as compared with that of licensed, that is, "chartered" state banks. Guthrie found the capital of private bankers to be at least $118 million, which was more than a third of the capital of the state-chartered banks. He went on to note, "The combined capital in chartered and unchartered banks being over $460,000,000, proves that banking is a favorite as well as a profitable business, and does not need chartered privileges to generate or protect it."[1] My own work on U.S. banking history in antebellum times led to an estimate of more than 700 private bankers operating in the country by the mid-1850s.[2] If the estimate is close to accurate, about one American bank in three was a private bank at the time.

Even then, however, private banking had entered a protracted period of relative decline that would in time lead to its virtual disappearance. Secretary Guthrie's statement to Congress that banking did not require "chartered privileges to generate or protect it" probably indicated that even by 1856 most people thought otherwise. Why?

Private Banking and Public Interest

There are, it seems, two possible sets of answers to the question of why banks ought to be licensed and regulated by governmental authorities. One involves public interest arguments. If banks are not licensed by government, then there is a greater probability that scoundrels and crooks will enter the banking business. And without continuing governmental oversight by government-appointed bank examiners, such bankers would mismanage or even abscond with the funds entrusted to them by the public. Since each bank is a component of the banking and monetary system, a few such "bad" bankers could undermine, even destroy, the whole system, which is built on confidence.

These are microeconomic considerations. But they have obvious macroeconomic implications. A "crisis of confidence" in banking could cause a monetary collapse and plunge the economy into depression. At the other extreme, unregulated banks might flood the economy with money in the form of bank notes and deposits created by making excessive loans. Unsustainable inflation would result before the arrival of the inevitable collapse. To prevent either extreme of too little or too much money from happening , the argument goes, governments must regulate banks to provide just the right amount of money for sustainable, noninflationary economic growth.

There are problems with these public-interest arguments. It is not evident, for example, why customers would deal with, or allow themselves to be victimized by, scoundrels and crooks in banking more than in other businesses that are unlicensed and unregulated. Moreover, it is amply evident from history, even quite recent history, that governmental licensing and regulation have prevented neither individual bank frauds and failures nor depressions and inflations. But here I shall only mention these still vigorously debated issues without further exploring them. The so-called public-interest arguments in fact had little to do with the decline of private banking.

The Political Economy of Banking

The decline of private banking had far more to do with the self-interest of both government officials and the non-private banks they licensed and regulated than with the public interest. The United States of the 1780s and 1790s was both capital poor compared to the West European countries and free of the English laws that required banks to be entities with unlimited liability and no more than six partners. In these circumstances, most early U.S. banks were institutions chartered by state legislatures as limited liability corporations. Attracted by limited liability, their owner-shareholders clubbed together their limited liquid funds to start the banks, through which they then made loans to each other and to non-owner customers. In return for their charters representing governmental authorization to provide banking services, the banks agreed to make loans to, and perform other services for, the states that granted them their charters. The states especially liked this arrangement after the adoption of the U.S. Constitution, for that document prohibited them from continuing the century-old practices of colonial, and then state, governments of issuing fiat paper money. Because of the Constitution, the states could no longer pay their bills by printing state paper money, but they could still charter banks that issued money.

The earliest state-chartered banks were thought of by legislators, shareholders, bankers, and the general public as public utilities. They were given exclusive privileges, namely monopolies of banking in their towns, in return for providing financial services to the state and the public. As the American economy grew and prospered, these state-chartered banking monopolies became highly profitable. Inevitably, new banks sought to enter the field to get their piece of the action, whereas those already in the field sought to keep out the would-be entrants. Resolution of these conflicting politico-economic pressures took several decades. The ultimate result in the leading commercial and industrial states was an American version of "free banking," which meant relatively free entry into banking provided the bank agreed to follow rules and regulations prescribed by state governments.

State legislatures and individual legislators thrived on the early American procedure of chartering banks individually by specific legislative acts. The grant of a bank charter gave the grantees a lucrative set of privileges not possessed by others. Bank charters therefore had economic value. The states and the legislators were not oblivious to this fact. They responded to it by charging the banks for their charters. These charges sometimes took the form of bonus payments to the states when charters were granted or renewed. They also took the form of bank stock issued to state governments on favorable terms so that the states could share in bank profits. Other types of charges included special taxes placed on banks and of state directives to the banks to finance out of bank resources certain institutions (such as schools) that the states deemed worthwhile.[3] These were above-the-board payments the states could demand of the banks in return for grants of charter privileges. These were popular because they kept down taxes on individuals. In addition, there were under-the-table payments to individual legislators for seeing that some banks received charters and that others did not. In state capitals, because of all these payments for privileges, bank chartering and state politics more or less became extensions of each other.

Enter the Private Banker

On account of all the political considerations involved in bank chartering, the number of chartered banks grew more slowly than it might have, given public demands for banking services. And for good reason. Charter values, and hence the payments that states and individual politicians could extract from banks, were greatly enhanced by restricting entry into banking. Restrictive chartering practices created a yawning gap for the private bankers. A demand for banking services was there, and growing. The chartered banks, the states' creatures, were not meeting the demand for politico-economic reasons that had little to do with economic efficiency. And nothing, at least for a brief time, prevented individuals and partnerships from plying the trade of banking without a license, just as private bankers long had done in England and Europe.

We do not know how many private bankers entered the field. Their numbers must have been large, however, at least large enough to annoy both the chartered banks and the state legislatures. The former had paid for their charters; the latter had received the payments. Unauthorized competition in banking threatened to undermine this neat political arrangement.

Hence, between 1799 and 1818, no fewer than eleven states and the District of Columbia enacted laws to restrict private banking. The larger states, where private banking likely was most vigorous, acted on more than one occasion. New York passed four acts to restrain private banking between 1804 and 1818, Pennsylvania three, and Virginia two.[4] The typical restraining act either banned private bankers from issuing their own bank notes, which was the primary method of providing bank credit at the time, or it laid a prohibitive tax on such note issues.

Such legislation served two politico-economic purposes. It reduced or eliminated competition for existing chartered banks, thereby raising the value of bank charters and the payments the states could extract for granting them. And it drove many private banks into applying for charters, so that they, too, would have to pay the tolls levied for governmental authorization to engage in banking.

Nonetheless, private banking persisted in the United States for decades. Privacy and minimal regulation were among its advantages, but the main reason for its persistence was that the states, and later the federal government, dragged their heels in chartering enough banks to satisfy the demand for banking services. American state governments and public officials were not inept in their slowness to charter banks. Both they and the banks already in the field had a financial interest in restricting banking development. That this interest was different from, and even inimical to, the real public interest was a small consolation to the private bankers. They were harassed by restraining acts and eventually driven out of banking or into "authorized" banking on terms set by government.

An Implication for Our Time

Although the private banker, with few exceptions, passed long ago from the economic scene, the history of U.S. private banking sheds light on quite recent events. In September 1994, the 103rd Congress enacted legislation to allow interstate banking. Thus, early in the third century of the republic, American banks at last obtained the freedom to do what flour millers, meat packers, and clothing manufacturers could always do, namely market their products throughout the country.

Why did it take so long? The fundamental reason, I think, is that in U.S. political economy banking is the last bastion of states' rights. Banking is the one area of regulated economic life in which the federal government almost always has deferred to the preferences of the states.

Federal deference to states' rights is unusual in American history. The Constitution transferred substantial but limited economic powers from the states to the federal government. During the first century of the republic, Congress and the federal courts used those powers to prevent the states from interfering with the emergence of a nation-wide free trade area. And during the second century of the republic, right up to the present, the federal government further weakened states' rights through federal laws, regulations, programs, and mandates that, for good or ill, increased the political and financial clout of the government in Washington relative to the governments of the states.

Given this record, how did the states manage until 1994 to resist the federal juggernaut and maintain their powers to regulate their own chartered banks as well as federally chartered banks operating within their boundaries, and to keep out banks chartered by other states? No doubt many reasons could be given. But underlying all of them must be this: Banking became the last bastion of states' rights because it was the first bastion of states' rights to matter in government-regulated economic life.

Early in U.S. history, the financial interests of state governments and politicians became substantially wedded to the interest of the banks they had chartered. Because banking was the first great corporate interest to be regulated in our history, state governments and banks together were able to resist encroachments into their terrain by outsiders in ways that later corporate interests, less regulated and less intimately tied to state financial interests, were not. Private bankers as a class were only one of the trespassers on the intertwined interest of the state-chartered banks and the state governments that chartered them. The first and second Banks of the United States established by the federal government were likewise trespassers. Like the private bankers, the two federal banks were beaten down and in 1812 and 1836, eliminated by powerful coalitions of state banks and state governments. In most areas the federal government discovered ways to override parochial state interest, but in banking it was itself overridden. Hence, the federal government learned the hard way to accommodate itself to state interests in banking, for a longer time than made much sense. The fragmented U.S. banking system, which continues to look peculiar when compared with the banking systems of other countries, is a result of the defeats suffered by both private bankers and the federal government in the early decades of the republic's history.

---

1. U.S. Secretary of the Treasury, "Report on Banks," (1856), 34th Congress, 1st Session, House Executive Document No. 102, p. 1.

2. Richard Sylla, "Forgotten Men of Money: Private Bankers in Early U.S. History," *Journal of Economic History* 36, March 1976, pp. 173–88.

3. Richard Sylla, John B. Legler, and John Joseph Wallis, "Banks and State Public Finance in the New Republic: The United States, 1790–1860," *Journal of Economic History* 48, June 1987, pp. 391–403, and John Joseph Wallis, Richard E. Sylla, and John B. Legler, "The Interaction of Taxation and Regulation in Nineteenth Century U.S. Banking," in Claudia Goldin and Gary D. Libecap, eds., *The Regulated Economy: A Historical Approach to Political Economy* (Chicago: University of Chicago Press, 1994), pp. 121–44.

4. Sylla, "Forgotten Men of Money," p. 182.

Free Market Money in Coal-Mining Communities

by Richard H. Timberlake

"In the company town, or mining camp, . . . United States coin and currency were not in good supply. . . . During the heyday of the old company town, scrip circulated more freely than U.S. currency and was indeed the coin of the realm. . . . Eleanor Roosevelt . . . in the mid-thirties, during [one of] her humanitarian crusades, attacked the use of scrip by coal mining companies as a very evil thing. . . .

Although many mourn the days of a bustling and active coal economy, little can be said to support the . . . issuance of scrip." (Truman L. Sayre, "Southern West Virginia Coal Company Scrip," in *Trade Token Topics*, reprinted in *Scrip*, Brown 1978, pp. 343–344.)

1. The Possibility of Free Market Money

Ever since the abolition of the operational gold standard in the early 1930s, the federal government through its agent, the Federal Reserve System, has been almost the sole creator of the monetary base, and has also been the licensing agent for banks that create most of the demand deposits used in the United States. No money of any significant amount can be created today without some sanction or act of the Federal Reserve System.

This condition has encouraged the notion that government is a necessary, or at least desirable, regulator of any monetary system—that without government any monetary system quickly degenerates into "chaos." If this supposition were valid, the evolution of money could hardly have occurred. The barter system that preceded early monetary systems, in which government had no part, would not have been superseded if the resulting monetary systems were destined to be chaotic. This logic suggests the possibility and perhaps the feasibility of a non-government money. However, the practical efficacy of such a system cannot be deduced from a theory that merely suggests its possibil-

Dr. Timberlake is Professor of Economics Emeritus at the University of Georgia, Athens. This article originally appeared in the October 1989 issue of *The Freeman*.

ity, but must be sought from historical evidence of monetary arrangements that have developed spontaneously in the private sector.

This paper examines one such incidence on private money creation—the issue and use of scrip, which occurred primarily in the isolated economic environments of mining and lumbering company towns during the first half of the twentieth century. Fortunately, numismatic collections and records reflect the operational character of the scrip system in these communities so that some evaluation of their monetary properties is possible.

Much of the recent research on the creation of private money has focused on that issued by private banks in the presence of a dominant legal money such a gold. (White 1984, Sylla 1976, Rolnick and Weber 1982) The issue of scrip, however, had nothing to do with banks. It was issued by private mining and lumbering enterprises. While it, too, was redeemable in a dominant money, its issue and acceptance were not critically dependent on any dominant money. For this reason, the phenomenon of scrip issue is especially revealing.

2. Legal Restraints Against the Issue of Private Money

Proscriptions against the arbitrary or casual issue of money appeared at the very beginning of this country's political formation. First, the Constitution stated: "No state shall . . . emit bills of credit, [or] make anything but gold and silver coin a tender in payment of debt." (U.S. Constitution, Art.1, Sect.10) No money except gold and silver was to be the legal tender issue of any governmental unit.

Money to be money, however, does not have to be *legal* tender. It can be what one might call *common* tender, i.e., commonly accepted payment of debt without coercion through legal means. Indeed, privately issued money to exist at all would have had to be common tender, and would have had to earn its acceptability in a market environment.

Even though the states and Congress were constrained to monetizing only gold and silver, the general laws of contract and commercial instruments sanctioned the appearance of moneys issued by privately owned commercial banks. (Hurst 1973) In addition, "Nothing in the Constitution barred private manufacture of coin, and through the first half of the nineteenth century Congress did not act against private coinage. . . . General contract law allowed any contractor to issue his notes and coins and circulate them so far as the market would take them." (Hurst 1973)

Free enterprise in the issue of common tender money was accidentally encouraged in practice by the federal government's ineptness in establishing a useful denominational spectrum of fractional currency during the nineteenth century. (Carothers 1967) Private transportation companies—canals, turnpike companies, and railroads—issued significant amounts of such currency between 1820 and 1875. Municipal and state governments did likewise. Redemption of transportation currency when called for was in services rendered, while state and local government currency was redeemed as tax payments. (Timberlake 1981)

The paucity of government-issued fractional currency was catastrophically aggravated by the first issues of greenbacks during the Civil War. The metallic values of subsidiary coins rose rapidly above their monetary values in the summer of 1862, and the coins disappeared from circulation. These circumstances provoked not only the ill-conceived issue of postage stamp currency, but also extensive private issues of minor coin. (Carothers 1967, Faulkner 1901) The act that authorized postage stamps as currency in 1862 also outlawed the private issue of notes, memoranda, tokens, or other obligations "for a less sum than one dollar intended to circulate as money or to be received or used in lieu of lawful money or the United States." (Act of Congress, 12 *Statutes at Large*, 592, July 17, 1862) Then in 1864, even the private issue of gold and silver coin was forbidden, again, "when the coins were intended for use as current money." (Hurst 1973)

3. The Appearance of Scrip as an Economizing Medium

The lack of adequate denominations in government-produced money was not the only factor that stimulated the private production of money. Shortly after fractional coinage was stabilized around 1895, coal mining and lumbering became major industries. Both coal mining and lumbering enterprises had to be organized in the vicinity of the contributory resources, so were often located in isolated areas with low population densities significantly distant form commercial centers. Coal-producing regions were hilly or mountainous areas where agriculture had been marginal and commercial development had lagged. "The 'Main Street,' " noted one observer in describing a coal mining community "was often railroad tracks." (Brown 1978) Coal mining entrepreneurs, therefore, had unique problems to contend with in organizing their enterprises.

Their common problem was what is known today as a lack of infrastructure—no streets, no schools, no residences, no utilities, and no banks or financial intermediaries. The specialized industries that might otherwise have provided these services were dissuaded from doing so by high start-up costs and the enduring uncertainties of dealing with low-income communities that might be here today and gone tomorrow. Alternatively, the coal mining companies could deal with such conditions because they were in a better strategic position to change incalculable uncertainties into calculable risks. (Fishback 1986, Johnson 1952) Mining companies, therefore, built residences, churches, schools, and water works, and opened company stores or commissaries. In so doing, they became both buyers of labor from, and sellers of commodities to, the coal miners and their households. This kind of organization invited an economy in the community's payment system—the use of scrip in lieu of ordinary money.

"Scrip" has become a generic term for the issue of a localized medium of exchange that is redeemable for goods or services sold by the issuer. Originally printed cards or "scraps" of paper, scrip evolved into metallic tokens with many of the physical attributes of official coins. Indeed, scrip in the very beginning was more in the nature of a trade credit, or demand deposit, at the single local general store. Ledger credit scrip, however, gave way to scrip coupon books, which "eliminated the tedious bookkeeping chores that were incident to over-the-counter credit (day book or journal entries followed by ledger entries)." (Brown 1978)

The use of scrip not only implied an issuer—the mining company—and a demander—the miner, it also required a supplying industry. The institutions that supplied coupon scrip were companies already in business printing tickets, tokens, and metal tags for various other kinds of enterprise. They advertised extensively in mining catalogues during the first half of the twentieth century touting the advantages of their own scrip systems. The Allison Company of Indianapolis, for example, noted that when one of its books was issued to an employee, "He signs for it on the form provided on the first leaf of the book, which the storekeeper tears out and retains for the [company] time-keeper, who deducts the amount from the man's next time check." Then, when the employee buys goods from the company store, "he pays in coupons, just as he would pay in cash and the coupons are kept and counted the same as cash. . . . The coupon book is a medium of exchange between the company employees and the company store." (from 1916 *Mining Catalog*, Brown 1978) Other scrip-producing ticket companies emphasized the safety of the scrip coupon system in coal mining communities "where little or no police protection is afforded." (adv. of the International Ticket Co., in the *Keystone Catalog* of 1925, Brown 1978)

The Arcus Ticket Company of Chicago advertised a list of advantages of scrip to both employer and employee, one of which for the employer was the fostering of employee good-will by avoiding misunderstandings on charge accounts. The advantages to employees included keeping the "'head of the house' better informed as to the purchases made by his family from day to day. . . . This frequently puts a check to extravagance and debt." (*Keystone Catalog* 1925, in Brown 1978) Local scrip of this type was very similar to modern day travelers checks. The cost of travelers checks were also the costs of coupon scrip: each unit could be used only once. It had to be signed out when it was issued and signed again when it was spent. (Brown 1978)[1]

The transactions costs of coupon scrip eventually encouraged increased use of metal scrip. This medium became cheaper overall than coupon scrip, in spite of metal's higher initial cost, largely due to the invention and development of the cash register after 1880. Pantographic machines were also instrumental in reducing the unit costs of metal tokens. (Brown 1978)

Instead of receiving cash, the scrip-issuing "cash registers" paid out metal tokens, made record of the payout and to whom it had gone and kept a grand total of the amount issued. The scrip registers would eject a specified "dollar" amount of scrip when a lever like that on a slot machine was pulled. In a 1927 advertisement, the Osborne Register Company (ORCO) of Cincinnati pictured a 10-year-old who, in demonstration, issued $600 worth of metal scrip in various amount to 200 hypothetical employees in 55 minutes, implying an average emission of $3 per employee every 16.5 seconds. (Brown 1978)

4. The Positive-Sum Benefits of Scrip

The economics of scrip issue, as with all exchange between economic agents, required that both the issuer (the coal mining company) and the acceptor (the employee) benefit from the transaction. The company necessarily had contact with the outside world. It bought machinery and other resources and sold coal in a national market. All of these activities required the use of standard money.

Scrip was used essentially as a working balance of money with which the coal miner could make advances to his impecunious employees between paydays. It was issued at the request of the miner to the extent of the wages he had already earned, and it was redeemable in standard money at the next payday. The amounts were usually small—five or ten dollars, or even less. To the worker it amounted to an interest-free, small-sum loan that he could get with almost no effort. It enabled him to buy ordinary household goods at the company store. To those workers who had "gone out and gotten drunk" on the previous weekend or had suffered some sort of household emergency, scrip was a blessing only measurable by the cost of its common alternative. (Clark 1980, Johnson 1952)

Its alternative in a conventional urban setting without scrip was the pawn shop, loan shark, or installment peddler. (Johnson 1952) An industrial worker in the same unfortunate position in, say, Detroit, Pittsburgh, or Chicago, had access to money in between paydays only by borrowing against his household capital at a pawn shop where he paid exorbitant interest rates if he reclaimed his pawned goods.

The scrip system could be abused in such a way that a discount would also appear in some scrip transactions. Since the company store did not sell liquor—for the obvious reason that its sale would encourage absenteeism and worker inefficiency—workers would at times obtain scrip from the company clerk and sell it for conventional currency in order to buy liquor. The bootlegger (during Prohibition) or other liquor vendor, whose shop was not likely in the neighborhood of the company store, faced significant costs in redeeming to scrip for conventional money, thus giving rise to a discount. (Brown 1978, Caldwell 1969)[2]

In spite of the obvious advantages of the scrip system to both worker and mine owner, scrip, the company store, and the company town have been universally bemeaned. (Brown 1978) The accounts of their operations include contradictions that appear sometimes in the same paragraph. (For example, see quote of Sayre used as an epigraph, p. 1, Brown 1978.) All accounts, while critical of the scrip system, acknowledge, first, that it was issued at the behest of the miner; second, that its issue cost the miner nothing; and third, that it was redeemable in standard money on payday. The dogma of the scrip's critics was that the company store, in which the scrip had to be spent, raised prices to monopolistic levels and thereby exploited the defenseless miner. (Dodrill 1971) Fishback's and Johnson's studies of prices in company stores versus those in independent stores refute this popular prejudice. Prices were four to seven percent higher, but so were costs. (Fishback 1986, Johnson 1952)

The advantage of scrip issue to the mine operator was that it was one worker perquisite he could offer to attract labor in a somewhat unattractive environment. He already offered housing and mercantile services; by issuing scrip against future wages he also provided commercial credit with virtually no interest charges to borrowers. (Johnson 1952) The practice, indeed, was so widespread that it can only be viewed as a traditional perquisite of the trade. A company that did not offer the scrip privilege would have been at a competitive disadvantage.

The mine operator thus became a quasi banker. His cost for metal scrip in the 1920s varied from slightly less than 1 cent to 5 cents a unit for scrip tokens of simple design made in aluminum. In brass or nickel silver and with scalloped edges and more intricate designs, costs could run as high as 11 cents a piece. (All of these values are unit costs in thousand-unit lots, and are from advertisements of several different scrip manufactures between 1925 and 1940, in Brown 1978.)

Scrip sales information from the Ingle Company sales journal of 1928 reveals that the average denomination issued was about $0.25. (Brown 1978) Since the average cost per token was only about 3 cents and could have been even less, an investment by the coal company bank in, say, 5,000 pieces cost it about $150 for the scrip coin, and perhaps a $100 or more for a scrip-issuing machine. To carry out this same banking function with regular U.S. currency would have required an investment in cash alone of $1,250, as well as substantially greater security costs to protect the money. One observer noted, "The mining company could pay almost its entire payroll in company scrip, disturbing only a few dollars of actual working capital." (Sayre, in Brown 1978) Of course, paying out scrip gave workers some additional claims on the working capital of the company stores. So the monetary economy of using scrip was in part offset by higher costs of merchandising goods.[3]

The difference between the payment system costs of scrip and of real money was a form of seigniorage revenue the coal mine operator realized and shared with his employees. They received interest-free loans; he was able to offer a fringe benefit that tended to reduce what would have been a higher working capital requirement.

While scrip was usually specialized to one company in a particular community, many coal mining companies had mines in different regions. Their scrip was good in all the different locations where their mines were located. As scrip-using communities gradually came to experience more extensive commercial relations with each other, their localized scrips became interchangeable. Even some independent stores accepted coal company scrip. (Brown 1978)

Given the proscriptions against the private printing or coining of money by the Acts of 1862 and 1864, one may wonder how scrip could have been used legally. The key is the word "intended" in the proscriptive laws. The courts ruled that scrip was not *intended* to circulate as money: first, because it was redeemable only in merchandise until payday; and, second, because it resembled money only superficially and was clearly distinguishable from standard money. (The coin under the courts scrutiny was a 50-cent token, but weighed only one-fifth as much as a standard 50-cent piece.) Any token that was redeemable in lawful money *on demand* was construed to be illegal, and whether the token in question was coin or pasteboard did not matter. (Brown 1978)

5. The Environments in Which Scrip Appeared

The extent of scrip use had many dimensions—temporal, geographical, and industrial. Its most notable occurrence in the twentieth century was in the coal mining regions of West Virginia, in part because the state government passed a "wide open" scrip law some time before 1925. However, it was extensively used in other states as well. The Tennessee Coal Iron and Railway Company, for example, ordered 547,500 pieces between 1933 and 1937 from the Ingle-Schierloh Company of Dayton, Ohio. (Brown 1978) Another source lists 20,000 coal company stores in the United States, Canada, and Mexico all of which used scrip between 1903 and 1958. (Dodrill 1971)

Numismatic records indicate that scrip was also used extensively in several other industries—fishing canneries, agriculture, (to pay crop-pickers), fruit canneries, logging and lumbering companies, and paper companies. (Brown 1978, Trantow 1978 Trantow's index lists over 1,100 companies that issued scrip currency in 40 states.) One scrip numismatist cites a Chicago newspaper of 1845 that regularly quoted the discounted prices of coal scrip, city scrip, canal scrip, railroad scrip, Michigan scrip, Indiana State scrip, and Indiana land scrip, as well as the notes of private and chartered banks. Private businesses issuing such scrip numbered in the thousands. (Harper 1948) Furthermore, as Brown observed, "the use of paper scrip was much wider than the use of [coin] scrip . . . [but] only a comparatively small amount [of the paper] has survived." Therefore, the extent of scrip use must have been much greater than the vestiges in metallic collections would indicate. (See also Caldwell 1969)

Just as Brown in his work seemed unaware of scrip that had preceded the issues by coal companies, Harper in his study of *Scrip and Other Forms of Local Money* thought that intensive use of scrip only appeared in the United States during the depression years, 1932–1935. His research uncovered several sources of "depression" scrip: (1) issues by local governments due to decreases in tax revenues; (2) issues by chambers of commerce after local bank failures as a means of "corralling as large a proportion of the depression diminished volume of business as possible for their membership"; (3) issues by "home-owned stores as a weapon against . . . chain-store competition"; (4) issues by "barter groups as a means by which the unemployed could more conveniently exchange services"; and (5) issues by charitable organizations to needy persons as "commodity orders" for foodstuffs. "Local money in some form," he concluded, "is likely to recur in response to a public demand under substantially similar circumstances."

Most of this "depression" scrip had appeared in earlier times—for example, municipal scrip that was redeemable as tax payments. The depression scrip, however, was usually linked to a dated stamp scheme that required the holder to fix low denomination (2- or 3-cent) stamps to the scrip at specified times. The stamps were to provide the revenue to redeem the scrip and to encourage spending, but they added an undesirable burden that greatly reduced the efficacy of the scrip's use. They also detracted from the scrip's effectiveness as an addition to the existing stock of ordinary money. (Harper 1948)

6. Implications of the Scrip Episode

The phenomenology of scrip issue has significant implications. First, no one had any incentive to leave scrip behind for monetary researchers to count or to analyze. Demanders of such currency would not regard it as a store of value for any time longer than the period between paydays. Suppliers, to whom the scrip was an outstanding demand obligation, would redeem it first if they liquidated, merged, or closed down their enterprises. In addition, everyone who used it and benefitted from it was aware of its questionable legality. Archival records of its outstanding quantities, therefore, are almost nonexistent. (Timberlake 1981)

Scrip's unrecorded existence is emphasized as well by the research that has uncovered its former use. Each scholar who has unearthed one of the diverse scrip appearances has treated the phenomenon as unique, and with a good reason. Each one is widely separated in time, place, and circumstance from the others. Yet, each one had characteristics similar to the others. All episodes combined emphasize the feasibility of the spontaneous production of money in the private sector.

The coal mining scrip episode adds significantly to the total scrip experience for a number of reasons. First, it lasted for over 50 years, so it was not just a temporary happenstance. Second, it appeared in a wide range of communities. In West Virginia alone, almost 900 coal mining companies employing about 120,000 miners issued scrip in one form or another. In other areas of Appalachia—southern Virginia, eastern Kentucky, eastern Tennessee and southwestern Pennsylvania—the experience was similar.

Third, scrip's tenure was not dependent on the previous existence of standard legal money. True, the coal company was bound to redeem the scrip on payday, but this guarantee was only a flourish that enabled scrip issuers to avoid violating the prospective laws against the issue of private moneys. As it was, many children living in coal mining communities did not see a dollar of "real" money until they grew up and left the area. (Caldwell 1969)

The self-sustaining nature of the scrip system, without recourse to standard money, stemmed from the fact that both the demander and the supplier of scrip were active participants in both the labor market and the household goods market at the company store. This intimacy in two markets by both participants enabled them to evaluate wages paid and received in real terms, that is, by the quantity of goods that the scrip wage could purchase. A decline in the purchasing power of scrip at the company store would simply have indicated to the miner that the real value of his services to the company had declined. He thereupon would have moved to another location or occupation. If the decline in real wages was due to an industrial depression or the competitive decline of the coal industry, as occurred simultaneously in the 1930s, both mine workers and mine operators would realize reduced real returns in the mode of any resource owners under similar circumstances.

A fourth important result of the scrip system was its reflective emphasis on the returns to the capital structure of the payments system. In the scrip system the money was supplied endogenously: the coal company banks, the borrowing miners, and the scrip suppliers were all parts of an economy of private ownership. Scrip money was not dependent on any outside money, but was produced under the same conditions and incentives as any common commodity. The mining companies rather than the workers produced the scrip because in working without wages until payday, the workers were implicitly extending credit to the company. Scrip issue was a means of clearing this debt before the regular payday. In addition, the coal mining company had the collateral value of the mined coal to secure the "loan."[4]

Both the companies and the workers realized the seigniorage returns from its existence. While the scrip system was small-scale and had a low profile, the government could ignore it because it posed no threat to the government's monopoly over the production of money. However, if scrip issue had shown any tendency to become a national practice, the prospective laws against private coinage would surely have been interpreted and enforced much more rigorously.[5]

An observer of the scrip system might conjecture that the experience of the isolated communities could have ramified into an intercommunity system using some kind of scrip clearinghouse (i.e. scrip banks) if the laws restraining the private issue of money had not existed. Over time technological and organizational developments could have led to economies of scale and enterprise. Some of the minters of scrip—Ingle-Schierloh, Osborne, Insurance Credit, Adams, Dorman, and others—would have expanded their enterprises to include management of intercommunity scrip systems and ultimately their probable evolution into credit card systems. Such an extension of function would have been analogous to automobile dealers expanding into the car leasing business—a short horizontal integration to reap certain economies of scale.

Had the scrip system become intercommunal and given rise to the scrip-on-deposit in scrip banks necessitating bank reserves and clearing operations, some high-powered scrip into which local scrips could be converted would probably have appeared. The experience of the ages seems to confirm this evolution. (Friedman and Schwartz 1986) Less clear is why the high-powered money has to be issued or regulated by the state. The question of whether or not the market system could, alternatively, produce a private monetary base that would prove to be both stable and serviceable has not been attempted or allowed, and will remain unimaginable until a general belief in market efficacy becomes pervasive. That time as yet seems nowhere near.[6]

Literature Cited

Brown, Stuart E., Jr. *Scrip*. Berryville, Va.: Virginia Book Company, 1978.

Caldwell, Walter. *Coal Company Scrip*. Montgomery, W. Va.: War Printing Co., 1969.

Carothers, Neil. *Fractional Money* (1930), reprint. New York: Kelley, 1967.

Clark, C.R. *Florida Trade Tokens*. St. Petersburg, Fl.: Great Outdoors Publishing Company, 1980.

Dodrill, Gordon. *20,000 Coal Company Stores in the United States, Mexico and Canada*. Pittsburgh: Duquesne Lithographing Company, 1971.

Faulkner, Roland P. "The Private Issue of Token Coins." *Political Science Quarterly* 16 (1901), 320–22.

Fishback, Price. "Did Miners Owe Their Souls to the Company Store? Theory and Evidence from the Early 1900s." *Journal of Economic History* 46 (December 1986), 1011–29.

Friedman, Milton, and Anna J. Schwartz. "Has Government Any Role in Money?" *Journal of Monetary Economics* (January 1986), 37–62.

Glasner, David. "Economic Evolution and Monetary Reform," (unpublished).

Harper, Joel W. *Scrip and Other Forms of Local Money*. Ph.D. dissertation, University of Chicago, 1948.

Hurst, James Willard. *A Legal History of Money in the United States, 1774–1970*. Lincoln: University of Nebraska Press, 1973.

Johnson, Ole S. *The Industrial Store, Its History, Operation and Economic Significance*. Atlanta: Foote and Davies, 1952.

Rolnick, Arthur J., and Warren E. Weber. "Free Banking, Wildcat Banking, and Shinplasters." Federal Reserve Bank of Minneapolis *Quarterly Review* 6 (Fall 1982), 10–19.

Sylla, Richard. "Forgotten Men of Money: Private Bankers in Early U.S. History." *Journal of Economic History* 36 (March 1976), 173–88.

Timberlake, Richard H. "The Significance of Unaccounted Currencies." *Journal of Economic History* 41 (December 1981), 853–66.

————. "The Central Banking Role of Clearinghouse Associations." *Journal of Money, Credit, and Banking* 16 (February 1984), 1–15.

Trantow, Terry N. *Catalogue of Lumber Company Store Tokens*. Ellensburg, Wash.: Trantow, 1978.

White, Lawrence H. *Free Banking in Britain*. Cambridge: Cambridge University Press, 1984.

The author is indebted for support and suggestions to the sponsors and participants of the Manhattan Institute Monetary Conference of 1986, especially David Glasner and Anna Schwartz. My colleague, Price Fishback, and Milton Friedman also made valuable suggestions, as did Houston McCulloch and two referees for the *Journal of Money, Credit, and Banking*.

---

1. This comparison must be qualified. Many travelers checks, as well as other U.S. currency, are currently used as hand-to-hand media in foreign markets. Sometimes travelers checks return from abroad with more than a dozen endorsements on them. They are called "checks," but like food "stamps," they are quasi currency.

2. Scrip was frequently advertised as redeemable only to the worker to whom it was originally issued. This condition applied in some mines. However, for metallic scrip, it could hardly have been enforced, and would have detracted from the utility of any scrip if it were enforced.

3. I am indebted to Huston McCulloch for this observation.

4. I am indebted to Huston McCulloch for suggesting these details.

5. In a thought-provoking paper, David Glasner argues convincingly that governmental assumption of a monopoly role over money enables governments to enhance their fiscal powers, particularly during war emergencies (Glasner, "Economic Evolution

and Monetary Reform," especially the section: "A Rationale for Government Monopoly over Money"). In short, not only is seigniorage an important revenue to the state, but capital expropriation through debasement of money's function as a unit of account may even be more lucrative.

6. However, the commercial bank clearinghouse system in the United States during the second half of the nineteenth century is an example of a private lender of last resort that produced base money efficiently at critical times. (Timberlake 1984)

The Growth of Privatized Policing

by Nicholas Elliott

Privatized police! The suggestion is usually met with disbelief, even by free-marketeers who would like most other government services shifted into the private sector. But there are good arguments to justify privatization of at least some policing functions, and few are probably aware of the spread of privatized policing that has been taking place both in the United States and in Britain.

Many object to private sector involvement in policing and criminal justice because they say that it is the state's responsibility to maintain law and order. This view fails to take into account the origins of rights. In liberal democracies, rights are considered to reside originally with individuals. The responsibility of law enforcement is only ceded to the state so that rights may be protected more effectively. The state does not own the right to enforce the law, it administers this right on behalf of the people. Therefore, there is no reason in principle why private individuals should not have law enforcement duties delegated to them, as long as they are responsible to the same system of law under which the state operates. This point has been argued by James Stewart, Director of the U.S. National Institute of Justice: "Although law enforcement is rooted in constitutional principles, the responsibility of government to ensure security need not necessarily mean that government must provide all the protective services itself."[1]

Those who argue against private policing often assume that it is only the police who ensure that laws are observed at all, that there is a sharp demarcation between the policeman and the citizen. This disregards the role that individuals have always played in keeping order just by going about their daily business. As urban analyst Jane Jacobs writes: "The first thing to understand is that the public peace—the sidewalk and street peace—of cities is not kept primarily by the police, necessary as police are. It is kept primarily by an intricate, almost unconscious, network of voluntary controls and standards among the people themselves, and enforced by the people themselves."[2]

Mr. Elliott is a financial journalist in London. This article originally appeared in the February 1991 issue of *The Freeman*.

A Growing Industry

Private sector police are nothing new. Until the middle of the nineteenth century most of Britain's policing was provided by groups known as "Associations for the Prosecution of Felons." These groups provided law enforcement, crime prevention, and insurance services to their members.

More recently, there has been a steady growth in the private security industries of Britain, the United States, and Canada. In each of these countries there are now more private security guards than official policemen.

More policing services are being contracted out to the private sector by the official police forces and by local government; and as private individuals become more affluent, they are showing more willingness to buy additional security from the private sector. There is evidence that private firms can often do the same job more efficiently and more cheaply.

All over the United States, different types of police service are being performed on contract by private firms. In Amarillo, Texas, local police have authorized a private security company to respond to alarm calls. Nearly three-quarters of American cities have contracted out the removal of illegally parked cars. A 1986 survey by Hallcrest Inc. found that 44 percent of U.S. law enforcement officials contract out the patrolling of public property.

In Fresno, California, 21 private security firms provide security at shopping centers, in apartment complexes, at concerts and sporting events, and at the city convention center and zoo. The firms provide their services to the city for $10 per hour, compared to the cost of $59 per hour if the police were to do the job.

Los Angeles County awarded 36 contracts for guard services between 1980 and 1984 and "county data show that the cost was 34 percent greater when the work was performed by county personnel."[3]

Policing functions frequently contracted out in the United States include prisoner custody, communications system maintenance, police training, laboratory services, radio dispatching, and traffic and parking control.

Other examples come from Europe. Private security firms in Bavaria are used to patrol the Olympic Park grounds, university sports arenas, a mental hospital in the suburbs of Munich, and the Munich subway. In Switzerland the private company Securitas employs 1,700 guards throughout the country to provide police backup services. Securitas has contracts with the police and with municipalities for such services as visiting restaurants and bars to ensure compliance with licensing laws, and patrolling parking lots and railway property. In the United Kingdom, a survey by *Police Review* found over 1,000 private security patrols in operation, including 239 patrols operated by private firms on behalf of local authorities.

Bromley Council in London was the first to use a private firm to patrol housing estates. The council hired Sentinel Security to provide patrols in crime-ridden areas.

Some local authorities also take on their own non-police security guards. At Livingston in Scotland, 42 council guards equipped with radios patrol housing and shopping precincts. The patrol is run by a former police sergeant who reports that "residents say they feel safer going out at night because of our patrols."[4]

A Further Stage

In a few instances, the whole policing of an area has been contracted out to a private firm. The first city to try this was Kalamazoo, Michigan. A private firm was given responsibility for street patrols and for the apprehension of traffic offenders for three and a half years in the 1950s.

One of the most successful examples is the small town of Reminderville in northern Ohio. Faced with having to pay $180,000 a year for continued county policing, residents decided in 1981 to hire Corporate Security Inc. for $90,000 per year. The firm also increased the number of patrol cars in the area, and improved the emergency response time from the previous 45 minutes to six minutes.

The private company was motivated to keep costs down because they were paid a flat yearly fee, and because they wanted to retain the contract. Adverse publicity for this radical experiment disturbed local officials who then set up their own town police department at higher cost in 1983.

Another example of fully contracted out police services is from Oro Valley, Arizona. There, fire-fighting, police services, alarm response, and paramedic operations were provided to 1,200 residents by the company Rural/Metro. The contract was agreed in 1975, with a flat yearly fee of $35,000 to be paid to Rural/Metro, a saving over what the same state services would have cost. Overall control of policing was retained by the town authorities.

During their time in securing Oro Valley, the company employed some innovative operating methods. They patrolled in four-wheel drive vehicles on difficult roads. They initiated a "dark house" scheme whereby residents who planned to be away could leave their addresses with the company, and their property would then be checked twice every 24 hours. Burglary rates in the area fell from 14 a month to an average of 0.7 a month.

However, the Rural/Metro contract encountered opposition from the Arizona Law Enforcement Officers Association Council, who refused access to training programs and refused to grant accreditation. When a state attorney questioned the legality of the arrangement, Rural/Metro decided to pull out.

Notably, when the town authorities took over full provision again in 1977, many costs increased. One change was to replace the civilian employees of Rural/Metro with uniformed officers on higher salaries. By 1982 the police budget in Oro Valley was $241,000 when Rural/Metro had done the job for $35,000.

Neighborhood Initiatives

In Britain and the United States, there has been a proliferation of neighborhood patrols, where residents take the initiative in patrolling their own locality.

On the Brunton Park and Melton Park estates in Gosforth, Newcastle, U.K., residents started their own patrol to deter thieves. Pairs of residents patrol the area in cars between 11 p.m. and dawn, reporting anything suspicious to the police. In three months of patrols only three break-ins occurred, compared to a previous annual average of 130. As a result, these residents have had their home-contents insurance reduced by 35 percent.

One growing form of private initiative in the U.S. is that undertaken by homeowners associations. There are estimated to be over 90,000 of these associations in the United States. According to the Community Associations Institute, 25 percent of them provide manned security for their members, and 15 percent provide electronic surveillance.[5]

In other instances, neighbors get together to hire security for themselves. Residents of a street at Blackfell in Tyne and Wear, U.K., hired a private security firm to cut break-ins and car thefts. One resident explained that "The police would come round after a crime was reported but usually could do little more than take the details from the injured party and offer sympathy."[6] Residents of East Graceland in Chicago hired a private security firm to drive out gang warfare from their neighborhood. They took on Security Enforcement Services for two months in 1989 for a charge of $8,000. Rather than strong-arm tactics, the company used intelligence to rid the area of crime. They became familiar with the known trouble spots and offenders, as well as with residents. They videotaped illegal activities such as vandalism and drug dealing, and then handed the tapes over to the official police.

The most unusual example of private initiative comes from San Francisco. The city is divided into 80 "beats," which are sold by the Police Commission to Patrol Specials deputized with peace officer powers (one step down from police officers). Beat-owners then seek business among the companies and neighborhoods in the beat area. The Patrol Specials must pass a rigorous selection procedure, before being sent on an arrest and firearms course at the police academy, and must answer to the Police Commission. The Specials cost nothing to San Francisco taxpayers, and they have endured since the 1800s.[7]

The private sector in law enforcement will continue to grow, and more individuals, neighborhoods, and local authorities will take the step of organizing their own local policing or hiring private security. The choice is either to encourage this as a supplement to official law enforcement, or to demand a rigid distinction between police and people. The experience of privatized policing demonstrates that the idea is not so unimaginably radical as might be supposed.

---

1. James K. Stewart, "Public Safety and Private Police," *Public Administration Review*, November 1986, p. 764.

2. Jane Jacobs, *The Death and Life of the Great American Cities* (New York: Vintage Books, 1961), pp. 31–32.

3. E. S. Savas, *Privatization: The Key to Better Government* (Chatham, N.J.: Chatham House, 1987), p. 183.

4. *Police Review*, January 13, 1989, p. 65.

5. Oscar Newman, *Community of Interest* (New York: Anchor Press/Doubleday, 1981).

6. *Police Review*, October 21, 1988, p. 3.

7. Christine Dorffi, "San Francisco's Hired Guns," *Reason*, August 1979; Randall Fitzgerald, *When Government Goes Private: Successful Alternatives to Public Services* (New York: Universe Books, 1988), p. 73.

Taking the Train to Metamora

by William B. Irvine

For a few dollars, one can ride a train from Connersville to Metamora, in eastern Indiana. The ride is worth taking not just because it is a chance to ride a train (which in America is now difficult to do), and not just because it is a chance to ride aboard a train pulled by a steam locomotive (which, as any train buff can tell you, is the ultimate experience in travel), but because of what the ride can teach you about economics, politics, and the way the two combine to shape the world around us.

Not long ago I took my family on the train to Metamora. Shortly after we pulled out of Connersville, I noticed the faint outline of the now defunct Whitewater Valley Canal running parallel to the railroad track. There was no sign of water in this canal; there was only a ditch with slumping banks and with rather sizable trees growing from the bottom. (The presence of these trees made it almost impossible to visualize barges ever using the canal.) From time to time, we passed the crumbling remains of canal locks.

It was only when I looked out the other side of the train that I realized that besides taking a train trip, I was traveling over a particularly interesting piece of the economic landscape. For on the other side of the train was a modern highway, being used by a variety of vehicles, including cars that had stopped to watch the steam locomotive go by. There, within the space of a few hundred feet, was a history of modern transportation: a canal, paralleled by a railway, which in turn was paralleled by a highway.

I examined the scene in much the same way as a geologist might examine a road cut (where engineers have cut through a hill in order to lay a road bed). To a geologist, a road cut offers valuable clues to the geological history of a region because it reveals the successive layers of sediment that were laid down by ancient oceans. Where the untrained eye sees a change in the color or texture of the strata, the geologist sees evidence of the rise of a new form of life, of changes in climate in years gone by, or of volcanic eruptions.

Professor Irvine teaches philosophy at Wright State University in Dayton, Ohio. This article originally appeared in the June 1990 issue of *The Freeman*.

The canal, railroad track, and highway, lying side by side, were the economic equivalent geological strata, but instead of revealing geological epochs, this economic landscape revealed successive revolutions in the technology of transportation, as well as revealing—to the trained eye—evidence of changes in the political climate in years gone by.

The juxtaposition of canal and rail and highway was also evidence of how dramatically the economic landscape can change. The people who built the canal probably didn't imagine that a technology would arise to make it obsolete, and the people who built the rails probably did so confident in the belief that theirs was the ultimate form of transportation.

By what, I wondered, will the highway be replaced? The obvious answer is that it will never be replaced, but this is what the canal- and railroad-builders thought. They were mistaken. Is there any reason to think that we are not likewise mistaken in thinking, as we often do, that we have reached the end-point in economic evolution?

Indeed, it is entirely conceivable that my children will tell their grandchildren about the old days when people used to ride around in cars. My great-grandchildren will listen wide-eyed and comment that things must have been difficult before they invented—I would like to be able to finish this sentence, but I don't know how to do so.

My great-grandchildren will most likely pity me for having to live without—again, I do not know what yet-to-be-invented something they will hold to be essential if one is to enjoy life. And why shouldn't they pity me? I pity my great-grandparents for having had to live without television and antibiotics and jet airplanes. Of course, I don't feel like a person worthy of pity; I don't feel like I'm missing anything, and I don't suppose my great-grandparents did either.

Only Change Is Certain

When it comes to predicting the economic landscape decades hence, only one thing is sure: It will be radically different—almost unimaginably different—from that of today. Generally, if there were someone who could tell us the future, we would not believe him. We instead prefer to believe those who tell us, in reassuring tones, that tomorrow will be like today, even though such people are almost never right.

The juxtaposition of canal and rail and highway also raises a number of questions: How does a canal or railroad come into existence? How does it die? Did this particular canal and railroad die natural deaths, or were they, in effect, murdered? And if they were murdered, who was the murderer?

As it turns out, the history of the Whitewater Canal is intertwined with the history of Indiana itself, and it is a history that demonstrates the extent to which politics can shape the economic landscape. (In what follows, I am relying on William E. Wilson's history of the canal, as related in his *Indiana: A History* (Bloomington: Indiana University Press, 1966).)

When Congress admitted Indiana to the Union, it allowed a certain portion of the funds from the sale of public lands to be used for developing transportation within Indiana. There were those, including Governor James Ray, who saw canals as a dying technology and favored instead construction of railroads. In the end, though, the state set off on a binge of canal and railroad construction, authorized by the Mammoth Internal Improvement Bill of 1836, and funded both by federal money and by $10 million borrowed by the state of Indiana. The Whitewater Canal was one of the projects thus financed.

The problem was that young Indiana was not ready to service the debt necessary to cover these appropriations: by 1839 the state was bankrupt. In the end, the state came up with a solution to the debt problem that was "just short of repudiation." The state got out of the canal-building business, and private enterprise finished the job that the State of Indiana had begun. By 1846, the Whitewater Canal connected Lawrenceburg with Cambridge City; the section of the canal between Connersville and Metamora is included in this stretch.

Once built, the Whitewater Canal's days of usefulness were numbered. By 1865 the Whitewater Valley Railroad had built the line that paralleled the canal (the line that the train to Metamora takes), and the canal was rendered superfluous. It wasn't long, however, before the Whitewater Valley Railroad itself fell on hard times. By 1877, it was bankrupt.

The Whitewater Valley Railroad recovered from this setback, but it ultimately suffered the fate of the canal: In this century, it ceased to be a commercially viable operation. What killed it? Again, this is a complex question. A case can be made, though, that in the same way that the railroad killed the canal by paralleling it, the modern highway—more precisely, the system of modern highways—killed the railroad. Furthermore, a case can be made—and many have made it—that the railroads died not because they are technologically obsolete (one need only look at Europe or Japan to realize as much) but because the government decided to nourish their competitor, the highway system.

In the early 1970s, the not-for-profit Whitewater Valley Railroad Company revived the Connersville-to-Metamora route as a train for tourists, and in 1984 the company purchased from Penn Central the track between Connersville and Metamora. Thus it was that I found it possible to take the train to Metamora.

On arriving in Metamora I purchased some railroad paraphernalia and took my family for a snack. The restaurant that looked the most promising was located in the basement of an old bank building. The problem was that the place seemed full. We were about to leave when a waiter came up and asked whether we would mind sitting "in the vault." I wasn't sure what he meant, but we followed him and soon found ourselves inside a long and narrow concrete bank vault. The place was barely big enough for a table and had a bit of an echo, but was nevertheless a treat. (I did experience some anxiety about accidentally being locked in—who, after all these years, would know the combination?—but my fears were unfounded.) No doubt those who built the vault would be as surprised to learn of the ultimate fate of their works, as would those who built the canal, those who built the railroad, or as we will be, if we are lucky enough to be around decades hence.

Private Highways In America, 1792–1916

by Daniel B. Klein

Fifteen years ago only technology aficionados and laissez-faire idealists entertained the notion of private highways. Today, however, public officials and entrepreneurs are struggling to make the notion a reality. Four private highway projects are underway in California and many other states are following suit.

The notion of private highways, which would seem fantastic to our parents, was commonplace to our great-great-grandparents. Initiated in the 1790s in the growing Republic, these roads stimulated commerce, settlement, and population. During the nineteenth century more than 2,000 private companies financed, built, and operated toll roads. States turned to private initiative for much the same reason they are doing so today: fiscal constraints and insufficient administrative manpower. Knowledge of our toll-road heritage may help encourage today's budding toll-road movement.

The Turnpike Heyday, 1800–1825

Once the state of Pennsylvania chartered a private company in 1792 to build a road connecting Philadelphia and Lancaster, rival states felt impelled to follow. Private initiative was the only effective means of providing new highways, because state and county finances were almost nonexistent and town resources were meager. Private control and user fees were bold steps, but once taken, states could only continue to move forward. In an age before the canal and railroad, legislators were willing to test community and political custom to get highways built.

The turnpikes were financed by private stock subscription and set up to pay dividends. Built with a surface of gravel and earth, turnpikes were usually 15 to 40 miles in length, and cost $2,000 per mile to build. They were massive undertakings and relied on widespread investment from the community. Stock purchased was more like a contribution to community improvement rather than a business investment. Some

---

Dr. Klein is an assistant professor of economics at the University of California, Irvine. This article originally appeared in the February 1994 issue of *The Freeman*.

Table 1
Turnpike Incorporation, 1792–1845

State	1792–1800	1801–10	1811–20	1821–30	1831–40	1841–45	Total
New Hampshire	4	45	5	1	4	0	59
Vermont	9	19	15	7	4	3	27
Massachusetts	9	80	8	16	1	1	115
Rhode Island	3	13	8	13	3	1	41
Connecticut	23	37	16	24	13	0	113
New York	13	126	133	75	83	27	457
Pennsylvania	5	39	101	59	101	37	342
New Jersey	0	22	22	3	3	0	50
Virginia	0	6	7	8	25	0	46
Maryland	3	9	33	12	14	7	78
Ohio	0	2	14	12	114	62	204
Total	69	398	362	230	365	138	1552

Source: Klein & Fielding, *Transportation Quarterly* (1992)

travelers objected to the idea of paying tolls, particularly to a corporate monopoly. Legislators, often suspicious of corporate motives, wrote extensive (and economically debilitating) restrictions into company charters, specifying conditions for construction, maintenance, and toll rates, and toll collection.

The progress of turnpike incorporation is shown in Table 1. Only Pennsylvania, Virginia, and Ohio subsidized their turnpike companies; New York chartered the most turnpikes. The opening decade of the nineteenth century saw the most charter activity, though roughly one-third of the companies chartered failed to construct a single mile of roadway.

The unprofitability of turnpikes soon became obvious. The vast majority of turnpikes paid only very small dividends or none at all. First, toll evasion was rampant, as people would circumvent toll-gates—a practice known as "shunpiking." Second, many roads were built in advance of settlement and travel demand was low. Third, legal restrictions and regulations, limiting both toll rates and countermeasures to shunpiking, hamstrung the turnpikes' abilities to improve their financial situation.

But poor financial returns did not necessarily mean unfruitfulness. Even an unprofitable turnpike stimulated commerce, raised land values, and aided expansion. Therefore, community leaders resorted to a fascinating array of tactics to boost the turnpike cause despite the sad prospects for dividends. Supporters used newspaper appeals, town meetings, door-to-door solicitations, and correspondence to apply social pressure. In this way as in others, American communities relied on voluntarism, as so elegantly described by Alexis de Tocqueville, to meet local needs. The result in terms of turnpike construction in New York is shown in Figure 1.

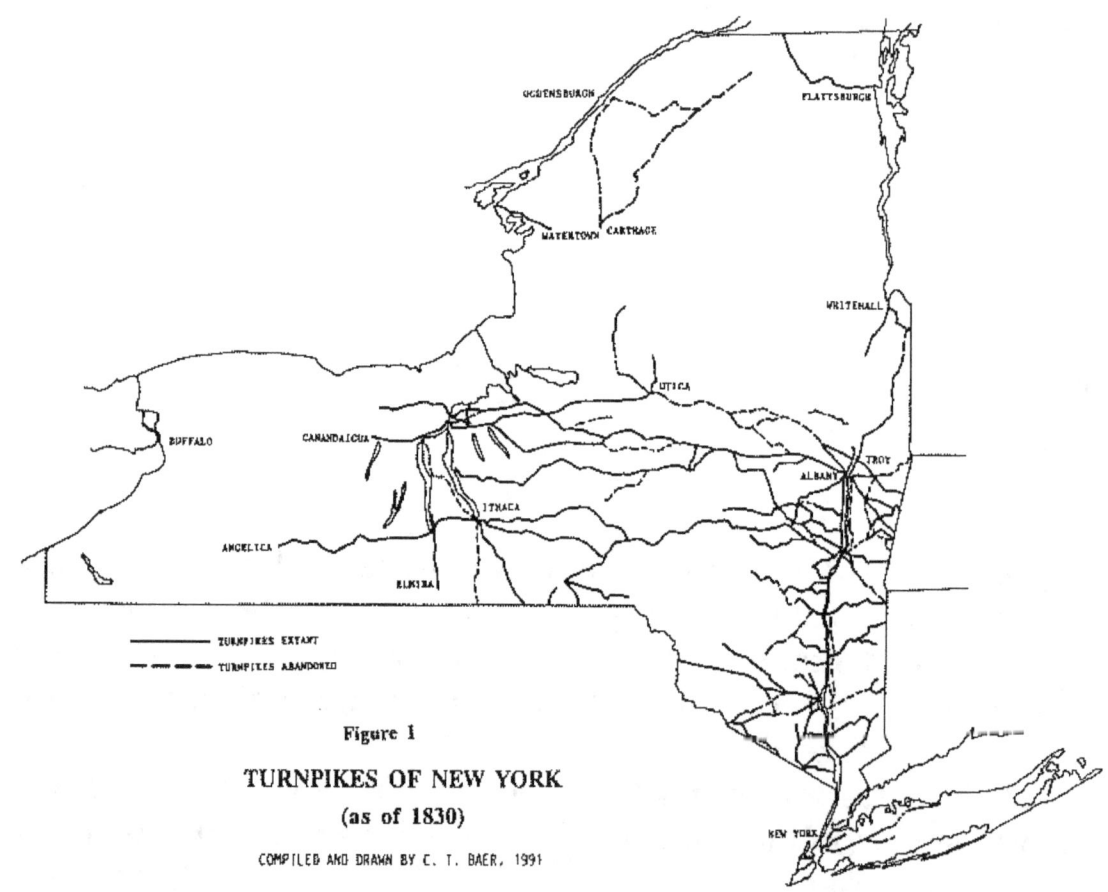

Figure 1

TURNPIKES OF NEW YORK

(as of 1830)

COMPILED AND DRAWN BY C. T. BAER, 1991

Canals, Railroads, and Spur Turnpikes, 1826-1845

In the late 1820s canals began competing with many of the major turnpikes. Railroads joined in a bit later. Between 1825 and 1845 turnpike mileage dropped considerably. At the same time, however, the canals and railroads changed the patterns of trade and development, and stimulated new demands for shorter toll roads that would serve as feeders. Table 1 shows that turnpike activity by no means ceased with the advent of canals and rails.

Plank Road Fever, 1847–1853

High hopes for a new kind of short feeder road were placed in the idea of plank roads, organized like turnpikes but surfaced with wooden planks. Plank surfacing promised a smooth, inexpensive alternative to turnpikes, which sometimes resembled a river of mud. Plank road fever struck in the late 1840s and thousands of miles of plank roads were constructed.

Civil engineers and enthusiasts predicted that plank roads would last eight years before needing to be resurfaced. Beginning in 1847, rural Americans financed and constructed plank roads in massive numbers. Table 2 shows total incorporation for several states. Figure 2 shows the plank road system in New York.

But the planks wore out twice as fast as predicted—usually within four years. The movement ended as suddenly as it had begun. Most plank road companies folded, while others converted their operations to gravel turnpikes.

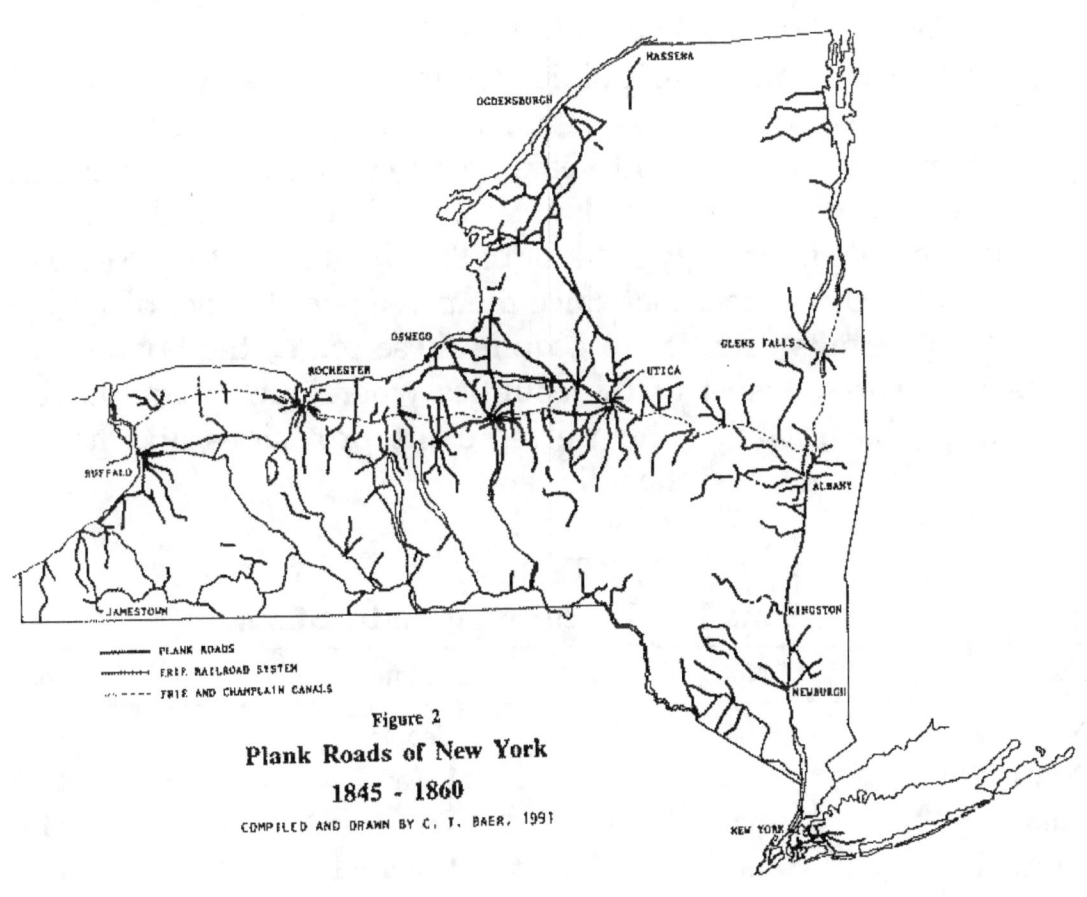

Figure 2
Plank Roads of New York
1845 - 1860
COMPILED AND DRAWN BY C. T. BAER, 1991

Toll Roads in the Far West, 1850-1890

The toll road idea endured to the end of the century. Discoveries of gold, silver, copper, and other minerals in California, Colorado, and Nevada sparked rushes of newcomers. Even before statehood for Colorado and Nevada entrepreneurs organized their own toll road enterprises to serve the mining communities, and some got rich in the process. Well over 360 toll roads were constructed in California, Colorado, and Nevada alone. This experience indicates that private initiative can provide infrastructure for economic development—so long as government respects people's liberty to do so.

The Good Roads Movement and the End of the Toll Road, 1890–1916

By the end of the nineteenth century, state and county governments had grown in capabilities and new agencies began setting goals for centralized highway management. Independent private toll roads were not thought appropriate in the era of progressive governance, and most of those remaining were bought out or shut down. Observed a county board in New York in 1906:

> The ownership and operation of this road by a private corporation is contrary to public sentiment in this county, and [the] cause of good roads, which has received so much attention in this state in recent years, requires that this antiquated system should be abolished. . . . That public opinion throughout the state is strongly in favor of the abolition of toll roads is indicated by the fact that since the passage of the act of 1899, which permits counties to acquire these roads, the boards of supervisors of most of the counties where such roads have existed have availed themselves of its provisions and have practically abolished the toll road.

Table 2
Plank Road Incorporation by State

State	No.	State	No.
New York	350	Georgia	16
Pennsylvania	315	Iowa	14
Ohio	205	Vermont	14
Wisconsin	130	Maryland	13
Michigan	122	Connecticut	7
Illinois	88	Massachusetts	1
North Carolina	54	Rhode Island	0
Missouri	49	Maine	0
New Jersey	25		

Notes: Ohio is through 1852; Pennsylvania, New Jersey, and Maryland are through 1857. Few plank roads were chartered after 1857.

Conclusion

In 1991 Congress passed the Intermodal Surface Transportation Efficiency Act (ISTEA), which changed the 75-year policy against toll roads. It permits the use of federal funds on toll roads, including ones designed, constructed, and operated by private groups. It sheds the old requirement that states repay federal funds if the facility is transferred to private control. Although highway financing should be strictly private, ISTEA greatly improves the present system, which relies on unpriced highways built and operated by government. Under ISTEA, America might begin to rediscover the effectiveness of private management and the economic virtue of user charges. With new electronic technologies of toll collection, toll roads make more sense than ever.

As we enter the potentially new era of privately managed highways, the historical experience with toll roads offers some important lessons. First, private operation is more flexible, creative, and motivated to serve than government control. In the nineteenth century, private road companies consistently out-performed their public-sector alternatives. Second, private roads will not be constructed without the prospect of private gain. If governments over-regulate or renege on their promises, private road development will not occur. Finally, infrastructure is an economic good best left to private action.

Private roadways have always made philosophical sense. Now even many public officials understand that they make economic sense as well.

Socialism, U.S. Style

by Henry Hazlitt

New York City's first subway opened in 1904. The fare was 5 cents. The subways remained under private ownership until 1940. The fare was still 5 cents. But meanwhile wholesale prices had gone up 32 percent; wage rates had tripled; the lines were granted tax exemption by the city. They petitioned for higher fares. But the 5-cent fare was sacred. The city fathers decided that the only way to keep it was to eliminate private profit and run the trains themselves.

So the subways were bought by the city in June 1940. On July 1, 1948, the fare was doubled to 10 cents. On July 25, 1953, it was tripled to 15 cents. Between 1940 and 1953 other consumer prices went up 91 percent, but New York subway fares went up 200 percent. The lines were still run at heavy loss. Even by its own method of accounting, the Transit Authority has lost money in seven out of the last ten fiscal years. If even one of its several subsidies from the city is deducted, it has lost money heavily in every one of those years.

The Transit Authority, which runs the subways for the city, is required by law to operate within revenues received from operations. This is a rather technical requirement. In the first place, capital funds (such as for subway construction, subway cars, and buses) are provided by the City of New York. There is a subsidy for carrying school children, and a subsidy for Transit Police.

In the fiscal year ended on June 30 last, the Transit Authority reported an operating deficit of $62 million. This deficit was achieved in spite of a tax subsidy of $166 million to Transit for the fiscal year. The subsidy was made up of New York City's outlays for all debt service, construction, and new equipment of $116 million; the subsidy for student fares of $20 million, and the subsidy for Transit Police of $30 million.

And now the fare has been raised to 20 cents—a 300 percent increase since 1940. The extra 5 cents is expected to bring in something in excess of $60 million, but probably will not be enough to cover the operating deficit even when all the subsidies are included. A 25-cent fare may be less than a year away.

This article originally appeared in the September 1966 issue of *The Freeman*.

As the charge for the service has been going up, the quality has been going down. The trains run less frequently; they don't meet schedules; they get older and dirtier, and so do the stations.

The Wall Street Journal recently complained in an editorial: "The change-makers in the municipally operated subway system refuse, usually with great rudeness, to accept a $5 bill or anything higher. . . . A person finding himself with nothing under $5 has no choice but to trudge back up the stairs and find a store willing to make change. Nine times out of ten the shopkeeper will do so in perfectly friendly fashion. The contrast is illuminating. The salesman in the store knows his livelihood depends on courtesy and service. To many a minion of bureaucracy, however, people are nuisances at best and to be treated as such."

This is "public" ownership. This is how socialism, U.S. style, works.

A theory has developed that municipal transportation ought not even be expected to pay its way. This theory is merely the outgrowth of government ownership. When cities own and operate the subways, the fare must be subsidized. When governments own the railways, the railway fare must be subsidized. When governments own the telephone and telegraph lines, the lines are subsidized. When governments own the power and the light companies, power and light are subsidized. When governments own the airlines, the airlines are subsidized. Governments run the mail service, and the mail is carried at a loss. Nothing is expected to pay its own way.

A subsidy on bread would be more defensible than any of these, but the government doesn't yet own and run the bakeries.

The socialist argument begins by saying that fares are too high because private industry is under the necessity to make a profit. What is overlooked is that it is precisely the need to make a profit, or to avoid a loss, that leads to economy, efficiency, and good service. Government ownership removes the incentive to all three.

New York's War Against the Vans

by Robert Zimmerman

In 1981, New York City had a transit strike. Only the Staten Island Ferry was running. Al Manti, a fireman living in Brooklyn, decided to help some of his local friends by driving them to the ferry so they could get to work in lower Manhattan. "We did it for fun," says Manti. It worked so well that he decided, once the strike ended, to buy a 15-passenger van and go into business. He contacted city and state agencies, filled out the appropriate forms, and received a license to provide transportation from Brooklyn to Manhattan.

Manti soon received hundreds of phone calls from local residents looking for an alternative to the city's public transit system. "I could've filled 50 vans, and still not met the demand."

Almost as quickly, he began to have problems with city authorities. The city held a special hearing and reduced his license so he could transport commuters only from the Bay Ridge section of western Brooklyn to Manhattan. Then the Metropolitan Transit Authority (MTA) organized a "crackdown on illegal van services." Transit police were assigned full-time to observe Manti's operation. One day he received 97 tickets. Sometimes the police would force Manti's van to the side of the road, and then give him a ticket for illegal parking. His family was put under surveillance. When he began to fear that the police would plant drugs in his vehicle and arrest him, he decided to fight back. He sued the Transit Authority.

The MTA countersued, claiming that his company was "damaging the agency."[1] For almost 10 years Manti fought the MTA, spending over $100,000 in legal fees. Instead of letting this beat him, he expanded his company so he could earn more money to pay his attorneys. "Sometimes," he says, "when I realize that I have spent more time fighting this battle than with my children, I have regrets. Yet I couldn't let the city do this."

From the beginning, Manti went out of his way to obey the law. He obtained a New York State Transportation Department license, followed its rules requiring state inspections three times a year, purchased

Mr. Zimmerman is a feature film producer in New York City. This article originally appeared in the April 1992 issue of *The Freeman*.

the expensive insurance demanded by the state, and obtained the proper licenses for himself and his drivers.

After almost 10 years, the courts ruled that the MTA had been harassing Manti. The MTA dropped its case and paid him $1,000,000 to settle. "If I had had an additional $100,000 to spend," he says, "I would have taken the case all the way and won a much bigger settlement. I just don't have that kind of money."

Throughout New York City, both legal and illegal van services have sprouted since the mid-1980s. Earl Simmons, Executive Director of the Jamaican Association of Van Owners/Operators, owns two vans and has operated them since 1987. "I bought a brand new van and started my business to get over the economic crunch," he says. Like most of the drivers, Simmons emigrated from the Caribbean, where private bus ownership is common.

New York's private vans, unlike city-owned buses, don't require exact change and will let passengers off at convenient points. Commuters who use them agree that they provide better service than the public bus lines. Typical comments include: "They're faster." "They're safer." "They're more reliable."[2]

By 1990 the vans were seriously cutting into the MTA's business, and the agency began another crackdown. In July of that year, the city announced a policy to enforce city regulations and to issue summonses for a wide variety of violations, ranging from driving a van that's not properly registered to improperly picking up and dropping off passengers. Fines ranged from $50 to $250.[3]

Transit police were assigned to the areas near bus stops, issuing summonses and preventing vans from picking up passengers. MTA police often issued large numbers of additional summons as a form of harassment. "Sometimes when they stop your van they would keep you there for a half hour," says Simmons. "Or they would stop your van and issue a *parking* ticket." In the first two days of this crackdown, two drivers were arrested and 60 summonses were issued.[4]

Even though many of the drivers had decided to obtain licenses, this crackdown was aimed at both the legal and illegal drivers. "Regardless of whether you are legal or illegal, you get harassed," says Simmons. "There is a direct attempt by the police department to issue as many moving violations to van operators as they possibly can."

Jeffrey Shernoff, a lawyer representing 14 van owners, points out that in trying to obtain legal licenses, "every one of [these owners] was strenuously opposed by the Transit Authority and all of the public transportation authorities on whose territory they thought [the van drivers] impinged."

According to New York State Transportation Department rules, privately owned vans can only pick up or drop off passengers by pre-arranged appointment, and cannot do so at city bus stops. Vehicles used to transport passengers are to have special licenses and be inspected three times year. The driver must have a special license and special insurance policy. A new state law specifies that only New York State insurance companies can issue this policy. Since there are only two New York companies offering this coverage, policies can cost as much as $8,000 a year.[5]

The MTA is quick to defend its local monopoly. "[The vans] siphon off our revenue," said Transit spokesman Termaine Garden in 1990, and in 1991 the MTA claimed that the vans diverted over $30 million a year from the public transportation system. Not surprisingly, the Transport Workers Union is on the side of the MTA, since they see private drivers as competitors. "They are brazen—grabbing people off the bus routes," says Pete Lynch, an assistant to the president of Local 100 of the Transport Workers Union.

None of this has reduced the use of private vans. In fact, when the city announced its crackdown in July 1990, it estimated there were 1,600 illegal vans. A year later, the city estimated there were more than 2,500. And of the more than $4 million fines imposed by the city, $150,000 had been collected.[6]

Because of police patrols, commuters and van drivers often have to sneak about to avoid detection. "It's like I'm buying drugs to go to work," says Wall Street lawyer George Freehill. And if police pull a van over, they often force the passengers off. Freehill relates one incident: "They stopped us on the FDR Drive, during rush hour, blocking traffic. They gave the driver a ticket for illegally carrying passengers. Then they tried to force the passengers to stay in the van while they weighed it, to give him another ticket for driving an overweight vehicle on the FDR. We all refused, getting out of the van. Then they gave him a ticket anyway for having an overweight vehicle, refusing to let anyone else see the scale. Finally, they forbid us from returning to the van, making all 13 passengers walk along the highway, which has no shoulder or sidewalk, until we could get back on the city streets to find another way to get to work."

Frustrated van drivers feel they are being denied their right to make a living. On October 14, 1991, a policeman issuing tickets in the Kings Plaza section of Brooklyn got into a fight with a van driver. The driver was arrested and his vehicle impounded. Other drivers responded by attacking several city buses, smashing their headlights and windows. In an attempt to free the arrested driver, they parked their vans in front of the police precinct, blocking traffic.[7]

The crackdown on private vans continues. Earl Simmons sums up a lot of New Yorkers' feelings: "If people elect to use these vans, I see nothing illegal about this. That is freedom of choice, that is the American way."

---

1. *New York Newsday*, August 21, 1991.

2. *The New York Times*, February 25, 1991.

3. *New York Newsday*, July 24, 1990; *The New York Times*, July 24, 1990.

4. *New York Newsday*, July 31, 1990.

5. Earl Simmons explained to me that if a van driver gets a lot of moving violations, the owner's insurance costs can skyrocket, effectively forcing him out of business.

6. *The Wall Street Journal*, July 24, 1991.

7. *New York Newsday*, October 17, 1991.

A Species Worth Preserving

by John Kell

What if you broke your leg in a tumble from a hammock? Would your pain and inconvenience be any less if you learned that few people break their legs this way? Probably not. You feel pain as an individual; knowing that total human suffering has increased only a tiny bit won't make you feel better.

Whether a broken leg is a major event depends on your perspective: Do you look at how it affects the individual or how it affects the collective? Public policies also can be examined from these perspectives.

For example, many environmentalists want wolves to be reintroduced to Yellowstone and Glacier National Parks, which are within the animal's historical range. Many ranchers oppose the idea because they fear that wolves will kill their livestock. Some environmentalists counter with the argument that wolves will kill less than 1 percent of the livestock in the affected area.

A fraction of 1 percent may seem small, and ranching as an industry wouldn't be greatly affected, but the income of a particular rancher could be seriously impacted. If a rancher lost a few head of cattle to a wolf, it would comfort him little to know that those were the only livestock killed by wolves in the whole state that year.

When environmentalists argue that wolves would have little impact on the livestock industry, they are thinking of the industry as a whole and not of individual ranchers. The rancher, on the other hand, is thinking about his particular herd and income. One is thinking collectively, the other individually, and each wonders how the other can be so unfeeling and irrational.

Is there any way these groups can come to view the problem from a common ground? What if environmentalists try to understand how wolves affect individual ranchers, and offer to compensate those who lose animals to wolves? This might help ranchers feel less threatened by the reintroduction of wolves.

Such a solution is being used by Defenders of Wildlife, an environ-

Mr. Kell is a biologist and writer living in Blacksburg, Virginia. This article originally appeared in the April 1993 issue of *The Freeman*.

mental group trying to reduce opposition to the reintroduction of wolves in Montana. They raised a $100,000 compensation fund through donations, a benefit concert by James Taylor, and sales of a print featuring a family of wolves above a geyser basin in Yellowstone.

Defenders of Wildlife has paid $11,000 in compensation since 1987. These didn't involve kills by reintroduced wolves, but were caused by a population that started naturally when wolves moved into Montana from Canada in 1979. Even so, Defenders of Wildlife felt the payments were needed to check the spread of an anti-wolf mentality.

Defenders of Wildlife hopes that the fund will be enough to run the program for 10 years. By that time they hope the wolf population will be large enough so the species can be removed from endangered status; shooting of problem wolves by animal control officers would then be permitted.

This isn't the first time that conservationists have turned to private funding to protect the environment. Ducks Unlimited, The Nature Conservancy, and Trout Unlimited have been buying habitat for years. But only recently have environmental organizations assumed financial responsibility for the actions of wild animals. The Great Bear Foundation in Montana started a program in 1985 to compensate ranchers for stock killed by grizzlies.

Like an insurance company, Defenders of Wildlife doesn't want to pay out more than it must, so they are educating ranchers to reduce the risks of losing livestock. They even bought a guard dog for one rancher who had lost cattle.

Environmentalists in other parts of the country are considering similar compensation programs. In the American Southwest, there are plans to restore the Mexican wolf. Conservationists have formed several coalitions and are trying to win public support for the reintroduction. Terry Johnson of the Arizona Game and Fish Department says: "A compensation fund is crucial to Mexican wolf reintroduction. Without it there is no hope for support or even neutrality from the ranching community."

Wolves seem to generate more animosity than the other large predators—grizzlies, mountain lions, and black bears—that run wild in Montana. The reintroduction of wolves is still opposed by many, and their future in Yellowstone is uncertain. One thing *is* certain. Environmentalists who are willing to bear the costs of their actions are a species worth preserving.

V. EPILOGUE:
FREEDOM THE *SINE QUA NON*

What Makes a Market?

by Ross C. Korves

Economists are quick to talk about markets, as if everyone knew what a market is and why markets exist. We talk about the corn market, the housing market, the insurance market, the baseball card market, and so on. Some people think of physical structures, some think of people shouting and yelling at each other, and others think of a list of little numbers on the business pages of the newspaper.

Recently some of my colleagues and I had lunch with a young economist from the Soviet Union. She had come to the United States to learn more about business institutions and how companies are organized. In the course of the conversation, we got around to the need for a market system within the Soviet Union so that communication can occur between producers and consumers. The prediction of Ludwig von Mises that socialism would fail because of the inability to calculate has come true, and changes are needed if the Soviets are to prosper. Even Communist economists from the Soviet Union see that.

Our guest agreed that markets are needed, but since none exist the government would have to create them. That sounded strange to me. How can a government create markets? We explained that markets develop spontaneously as people interact. As people freely act they sort out what they want and don't want, and they communicate these ideas back to suppliers. But she didn't appear to be able to grasp that markets spring up on their own. We mentioned the black market within her own country as an example of people creating a market as the need developed. That didn't seem to connect. She came back to the point that no markets existed, and the government would have to create them.

After a while, I concluded that the Soviet economist lacked an appreciation for freedom, particularly the freedom for individual consumers to communicate their wishes through a market system. Markets develop as hundreds and thousands of individuals make their wishes known. But Communism is a top-down system. Decisions on

Mr. Korves is Economist and Chief Policy Analyst, Economic Research Division, American Farm Bureau Federation. This article originally appeared in the September 1990 issue of *The Freeman*.

what to produce are made at the top, and consumers are forced to live with those decisions. The idea of consumer sovereignty doesn't exist. The more I thought about, the more it became obvious that their consumers cannot be thought of as making decisions because in the Communist system there is no freedom. Individuals don't exist of and by themselves. Only the state exists, and people are just part of the larger system.

The freedom to act is fundamental to the development of a market. Some friends of mine are in the property casualty reinsurance business. Having had substantial claims as a result of Hurricane Hugo, they devised a way to calculate the additional coverage that would be needed if a similar catastrophe were to happen in the future. They took their proposal to "the market" and found that the reinsurance industry could easily understand what they were trying to do and quickly established a value on the activity. But without the freedom to act on an idea, and the freedom for others to react, there would be no market for that type of reinsurance.

This "market" that the reinsurer went to doesn't exist in a physical sense. There is no building. There was no group of people shouting at each other in a large pit. And I didn't find a listing of prices in *The Wall Street Journal* the following day. If the government had set out to create this market for reinsurance, there would have been nothing to create. It was all in the heads of the people who sought out the reinsurance and those who responded to that need. There were, eventually, papers to be signed and accounts to be established but that came after the market was established. If this type of reinsurance becomes popular enough, something about it may eventually be listed daily on the financial pages. To go one step further, if this reinsurance became extremely common, maybe an insurance exchange building would be built to put all the people involved in this market in the same place to make market activity easier. A lot of business people and individual buyers would use the market. At that point, undoubtedly, some local, state, or federal government politician or agency would want to regulate the market to protect the participants from their own freedom of association.

I am not sure that the young Soviet economist ever grasped what we tried to explain about markets springing forth from the actions of individuals using their freedom to make choices. But I learned one more time that personal freedom is the basis for markets. Where there is no freedom, there are no markets, regardless of what a government may try to create.

Index

Addams, Jane, 70
Allen, William R., 25-27
American Revolution, 44
American Civil Liberties Union, 39
American Nazi Party, 39
Ancient Order of Foresters, 88
Anti-Semitism, 39-40
Arizona Game and Fish Department, 141
Arizona Law Enforcement Officers Association Council, 122
Art: in ancient Egypt, 30; in ancient Rome 31; commercial, 28; fine, 28, 32; government influences, 25-27; in the Soviet Union, 31

Bank of New York, 100
Bank of the United States, 105
Bankers, 99-105
Bastiat, Frederic, 14
Bavaria, 120
Bazikian, Daniel A., 68-71
Beito, David, T., 87-95
Best, Samuel, 83
Billboards: aesthetic concerns, 34; free speech aspects, 35; and environmentalists, 34; government regulation of, 34
Black, Hugo, 48
Black Death, 32
Bolick, Clint, 44-53
Broadway Presbyterian Church, 75
Brown Brothers Harriman, 100
Building societies, 84
Burial societies, 84

Cable television, 44
Charitable laws, in Tudor England, 66
Charity, see Philanthropy

Chodes, John, 81-85
Christenson, Richard, 66-67
Civil War, 108
Collins, Marva, 62, 63
Combinations Acts, 85
Communism, 145
Cornuelle, Richard, 1
Czechoslovak Society of America, 82

De Sola Pool, Ithiel, 46, 53
Defenders of Wildlife, 140, 141
Defoe, Daniel, 81
Deregulation, 41
Dickneider, William, 25-27
Dictionary of the English Language, 23
Direct broadcast satellites, 45
Dividing societies, 82, 83
Dodsworth, Barbara, 28-32
Douglas, William O., 52-53
Ducks Unlimited, 141
Duerer, Albrecht, 32
DuPont, Alfred, 78, 80

Economic growth, 15
Economic planning: bureaucracy and, 12; under Communism, 10; in Germany, 17; in France, 16, 17; the private sector and, 13; the public sector and, 13; in the Soviet Union, 15; the welfare state and, 14; in World War II, 11
Edison, Thomas, 3
Education, 57-61, 62
Elizabeth, Queen of England, 66
Elliott, Nicholas, 119-123

Factory Societies, 84
Fargo, John, 72-74
Farhat, Marina, 63, 64, 65

Federal Communications Commission, 45
Federal Reserve System, 109
Female Union Band, 89
Finneran, John P., 21-24
Flintstone, Fred, 87
Food, regulation of, 36-40
Foresters, 88
Fraternal Order of the Deaf, 82
Fraternal Order of Eagles, 88
Fraternal societies, 85
Freeman (The), 2
Free speech, commercial; regulation of, 48, 49
French Academy, 2, 22; dictionary of, 24
Friendly societies, 81-85
Furetière, Antoine, 22, 24

Galbraith, J.K., 10, 13, 14
Garrick, David, 24
Gasman, Lawrence, 41-43
Generosity of Americans (Marts), 66-67
Gilder, George, 43
Girad, Stephen, 100
Glacier National Park, 140
Goldwater, S.S, 87-88, 92
Great Depression, 95, 72
Great Society, 71
Greeley, Horace, 70
Greenbacks, 108
Guthrie, James, 100

Hamilton, Alexander, 99
Hazlitt, Henry, 9-17, 134-135
Health care, *see* Medical care
Heightened Options in Private Education, 62-65
Henry VIII, King of England, 66
Hitchen Friendly Institution, 83
Holy Ghost, 89
Home Schooling: advantages of, 61; difficulties of, 57, 58; legal challenges to, 60; methods of, 60
Huber, Peter, 43

HOPE Academy, 62-65
Humanism, 31
Hurricane Hugo, 146

Illegal Societies Act, 85
Indiana: A History (Wilson), 126
Intermodal Surface Transportation Efficiency Act (1991), 133
Irvine, William B., 124-127

Jacobs, Jane, 119
Jefferson, Thomas, 48, 53
Johnson, Lyndon, 71
Johnson, Samuel, 2, 21, 22, 23
J. P. Morgan and Company, 100
Julius II, Pope, 29
Juvenal, 23

Kashrus Magazine, 37
Kashrut, see Kosher regulation
Keating, Raymond J., 41-43
Kell, John, 140-141
Klein, Daniel B., 128-133
Kosher regulation, 36, 37, 38, 40
Kramden, Ralph, 87

Ladies Friends of Faith, 89
Lapp, Hannah, 57-61
Locomotive Engineers Mutual Life and Accident Insurance Association, 82
Lodge practice, 91
Lord Chesterfield, 23
Louis XIII, King of France, 21

Madison, James, 53
Mammoth Internal Improvement Bill (1836), 126
Mandela, Nelson, 35
Manhattan, 135
Mann, Horace, 4
Manti, Al, 136
Markets, 145-146
Marshall Plan, 16
Marshall, Thurgood, 48

Martineau, Harriet, 67
Marts, Arnaud C., 66-67
Mashgichim, 38
Mathews, George S., 92
McClure's Magazine, 88
McManemin, John C., 92
Medical care, 78-79, 91
Medical schools, 93
Metropolitan Museum of Art, 29
Michelangelo, 29
Mises, Ludwig von, 49, 145
Mixon, J. Wilson, Jr., 1-6
Money, 106-118. *See also* Bankers
Monopolies, 50
Morgan Guaranty Trust Company, 16-17
Mother's Day, 89
Multi-point distribution service, 45

Nash, Ogden, 33-34
National Insurance Act (1911), 85
Nature Conservancy, 141
Nemours Foundation, 79, 80
New Deal, 70
New York City: subways, 134; Transit Police, 134
New York State Transportation Department, 136
New York Tribune, 69

Ojeda, Mova, 77
Olasky, Marvin, 68-71
O'Neill, Tip, 81
Orwell, George, 46, 47, 48, 52

Patrol Specials, 123
Payne, Scott, 62-65
Person, Lawrence, 33-35
Peterson, Robert A., 78-80
Philanthropy, 66-71; of farmers, 72-74
Photography, 28
Pierce, Zachary, 23
Plank roads, 130
Police Review, 121
Policing, private, 119-123

Policy Review, 75
Poor Laws, of England, 4
Presbyterian Church (U.S.A.), 76
Press, freedom of, 47-48, 50-51
Private banking: extent of, 100; and political economy, 101, 102; and public interest, 101; and U.S. Constitution, 102
Private highways, 128-133
Private policing, 119-123; growth of, 120
Prohibition, 111
Providence Association of the Ukrainian Catholics in America, 82
Public access, 51

Rabbinical Council of California, 39
Read, Leonard E., 1
Relief: indoor, 69; outdoor, 69
Renaissance, 29, 30, 31
Roads, 128-133
Roosevelt, Eleanor, 106
Rose Act, 85
Rural/Metro, 121-122

Sambaer, Eleanor, 62
Scarcity, 50
Schlesinger, A.M., Sr., 67
Schmidt, Helmut, 46
Scrip, 106-118; appearance of, 108; benefits of, 110; implications of, 114
Scrip and Other Forms of Local Money (Harper), 113
Seditious Meetings Act, 85
Shunpiking, 129
Smith, Ralph Lee, 45
Social Darwinism, 69-70
Social Universalism, 70
Soviet Union, 145
Staten Island, 136
Stewart, Potter, 48
Sullum, Jacob, 36-40
Switzerland, 120
Sylla, Richard, 99-105

Teaching Home, 61
Technologies of Freedom (de Sola Pool), 46
Telecommunications, 41-43, 44-56
Telecompetition: The Free Market and the Road to the Information Superhighway (Gasman), review of, 41-43
Tennessee Coal Iron and Railway Company, 113
Timberlake, Richard H., 106-118
Tocqueville, Alexis de, 130
Toll roads, 131
Tragedy of American Compassion (Olasky), 68-71
Train travel: economic aspects of, 125
Trout unlimited, 141
Turnpikes, 128

U.S. Constitution: Amendment I, 48, 51, 52; Art. 1 Sect. 10, 107; and banking, 104
U.S. National Institute of Justice, 119
U.S. Supreme Court, 50

Union Theological Seminary, 75
Union Provident Sick Society, 83
United Sons and Daughters, 89

Virginia Declaration of Rights, 47

Wall Street Journal, 135, 146
Washington Post, 37, 39
Welfare, 75-79
Whitewater canal, 126
Whitewater Valley Railroad, 126
Wiley, W. L., 22
Wilson, William E., 126
Wired Nation (Smith), 45
Wisconsin Journal of Medicine, 90
Wisz, Gerald, 75-77

Yellowstone National Park, 140
Young Men of Inseparable Friends, 89

Zenger, John Peter, 48
Zierath, W.F., 90, 91, 94

About the Publisher

The Foundation for Economic Education, Inc., was established in 1946 by Leonard E. Read to study and advance the moral and intellectual rationale for a free society.

The Foundation publishes *The Freeman*, an award-winning monthly journal of ideas in the fields of economics, history, and moral philosophy. FEE also publishes books, conducts seminars, and sponsors a network of discussion clubs to improve understanding of the principles of a free and prosperous society.

FEE is a non-political, non-profit 501(c)(3) tax-exempt organization, supported solely by private contributions and sales of its literature.

For further information, please contact: The Foundation for Economic Education, Inc., 30 South Broadway, Irvington-on-Hudson, New York 10533. Telephone (914) 591-7230; fax (914) 591-8910.